# Cobourg Ontario Book 1 in Colour Photos, Saving Our History One Photo at a Time

Photography
by Barbara Raué
©2019

Series Name: Cruising Ontario

Book 225: Cobourg Book 1

Cover photo: 351 William Street, Page 66

# Series Name: Cruising Ontario
## Saving Our History One Photo at a Time
## in colour photos

Books Available in Alphabetical Order:
Aberfoyle, Acton, Ajax, Alton, Amherstburg, Ancaster, Arthur, Auburn, Aylmer, Ayr, Beaver Valley, Belgrave, Belleville, Bloomingdale, Blyth, Brantford, Brockville, Burford, Burlington, Caledon, Caledonia, Cambridge, Carlow, Chatsworth, Clifford, Collingwood, Conestogo, Delhi, Dorchester to Aylmer, Drayton, Drumbo, Dundas, Dunlop, Eden Mills, Elmira, Elora, Erin, Essex, Fergus, Goderich, Grimsby, Guelph, Hagersville, Hamilton, Hanover, Harriston, Hespeler, Jarvis, Kingston, Kingsville, Kitchener, Lake Superior, Lincoln, Linwood, Listowel, London, Lucknow, Merrickville, Mono, Mount Forest, Mount Pleasant, Neustadt, New Hamburg, Newboro, Newport, Niagara-on-the-Lake, Niagara Falls, North Bay, Oakville, Onondaga, Orangeville, Orillia, Oshawa, Owen Sound, Palmerston, Paris, Pelham, Perth, Peterborough, Petrolia, Pickering, Port Colborne, Port Elgin, Portland, Preston, Rockwood, Sarnia, Sault Ste. Marie, Seaforth, Sheffield, Shelburne, Simcoe, Smiths Falls, Smithville, Southampton, St. Catharines, St. George, St. Jacobs, St. Marys, St. Thomas, Stoney Creek, Stratford, Thamesford, Thunder Bay, Tillsonburg, Toronto, Waterdown, Waterford, Waterloo, Welland, Wellesley, West Flamborough, Westport, Whitby, Windsor, Wingham, Woodstock

Book 212-215 Haldimand County
Book 216: Sudbury
Book 217: Parry Sound
Book 218-219: Uxbridge
Book 220: Port Perry

Book 221-222: Stouffville
Book 223: Colborne
Book 224: Grafton, Bolton
Book 225-229: Cobourg

# Table of Contents

King Street West                    Page 5

King Street East                    Page 42

Fitzhugh Lane                       Page 63

William Street                      Page 65

Cobourg is a town in Southern Ontario ninety-five kilometers (59 miles) east of Toronto and 62 kilometers (39 miles) east of Oshawa. It is located along Highway 401. To the south, Cobourg borders Lake Ontario.

The settlements that make up today's Cobourg were founded by United Empire Loyalists in 1798. The Town was originally a group of smaller villages such as Amherst and Hardscrabble, which were later named Hamilton. In 1808 it became the district town for the Newcastle District. It was renamed Cobourg in 1818, in recognition of the marriage of Princess Charlotte Augusta of Wales to Prince Leopold of Saxe-Coburg-Saalfeld (who later become King of Belgium).

By the 1830s Cobourg had become a regional center, much due to its fine harbor on Lake Ontario. In 1835 the Upper Canada Academy was established in Cobourg by Egerton Ryerson and the Wesleyan Conference of Bishops. On July 1, 1837, Cobourg was officially incorporated as a town. In 1841 the Upper Canada Academy's name was changed to Victoria College. In 1842 Victoria College was granted powers to confer degrees.

Cobourg retains its small-town atmosphere, in part due to the downtown and surrounding residential area's status as a Heritage Conservation District. The downtown is a well-preserved example of a traditional small-town main street. Victoria Hall, the town hall completed in 1860, is a National Historic Site of Canada. The oldest building in the town is now open as the Sifton-Cook Heritage Centre and operated by the Cobourg Museum Foundation.

Food processing is the largest industry in Cobourg, and it is home to SABIC Innovative Plastics and Weetabix.

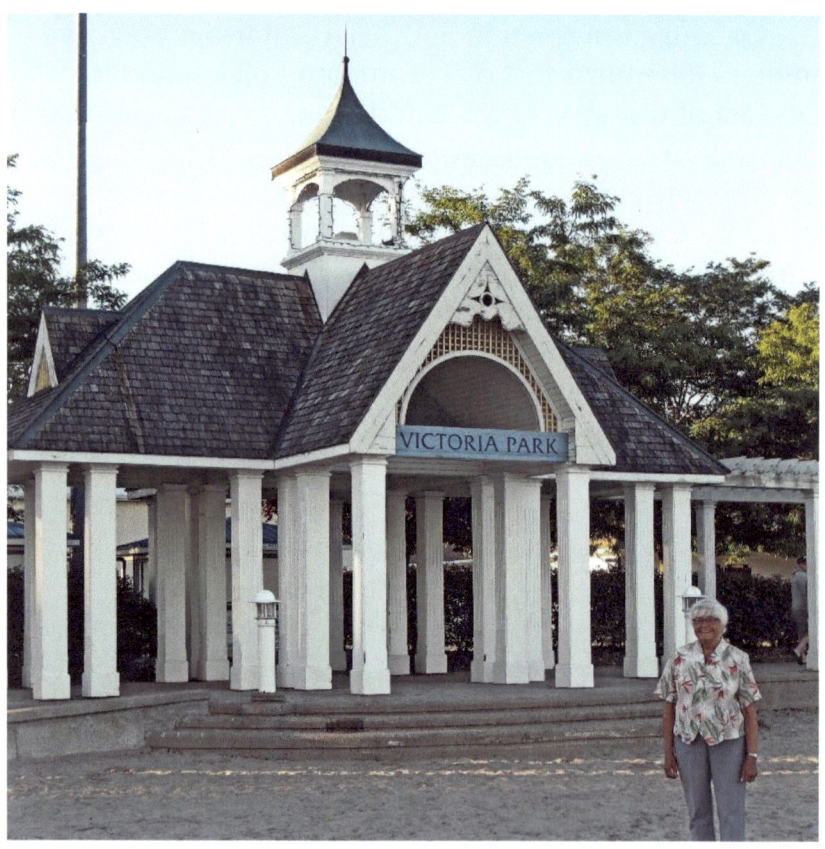

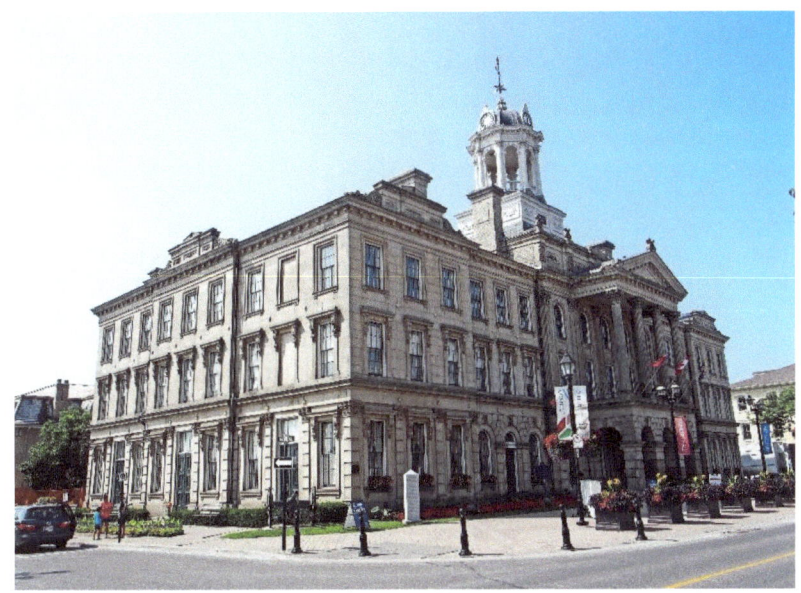

55 King Street West – Victoria Hall – 1860 – It is in the Palladian Neo-Classical architectural style with Corinthian capitals on the fluted columns and pilasters decorating the façade. The building is topped with a massive clock tower with Corinthian columns. On the first floor is a courtroom, and a concert hall on the second floor.

Standing at the heart of the downtown is Victoria Hall, a building that now serves as the town hall, as well as home of the Art Gallery of Northumberland, the Cobourg Concert Hall, and an Old-Bailey-style courtroom that is now used as the Council chamber. Victoria Hall is a landmark known for its impressive stone work. Charles Thomas (1820-1867), an English-born master stone carver and building contractor, executed the fine stone carvings, including the bearded faced keystone over the main entrance into the building. Victoria Hall was officially opened in 1860 by the Prince of Wales, later to become King Edward VII of the United Kingdom.

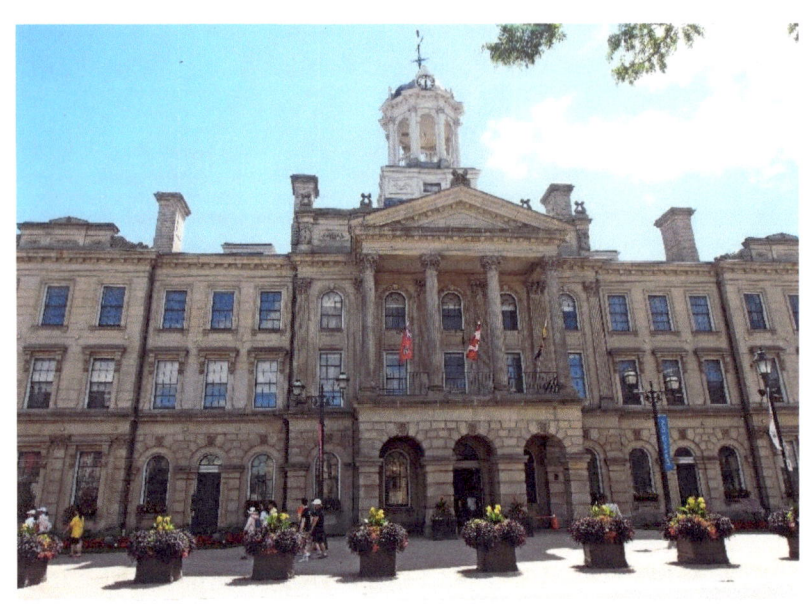

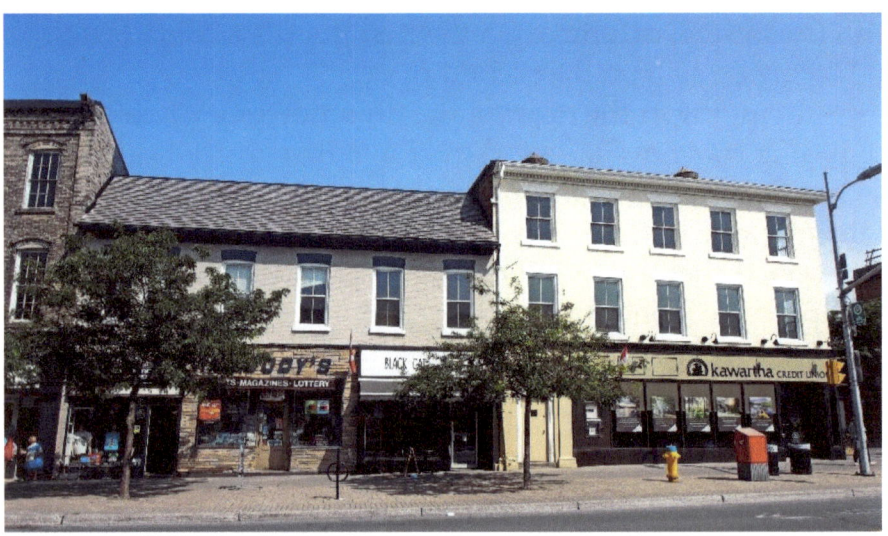

2-10 King Street West

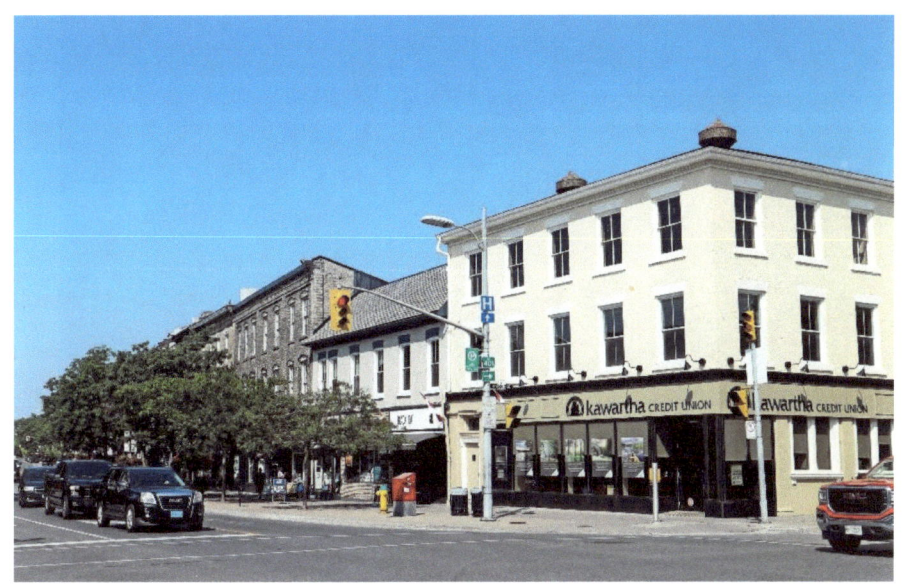

2 King Street West

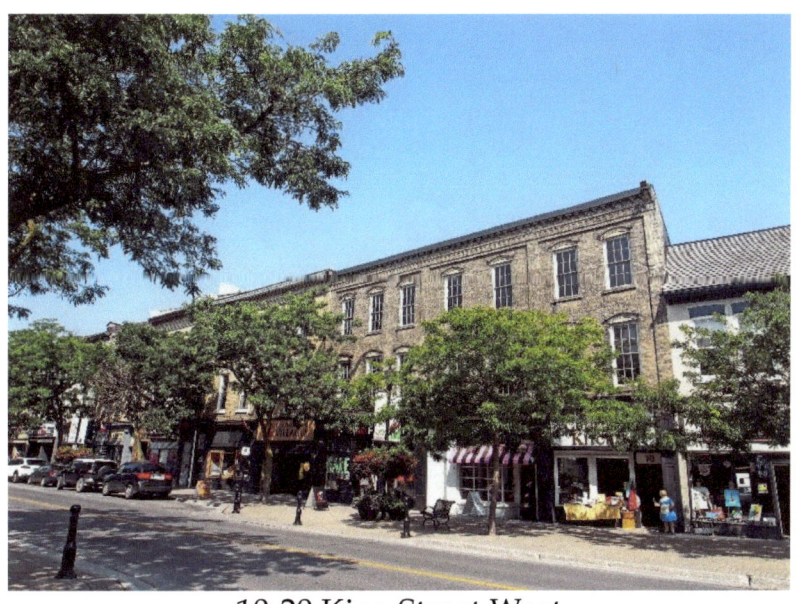

10-20 King Street West

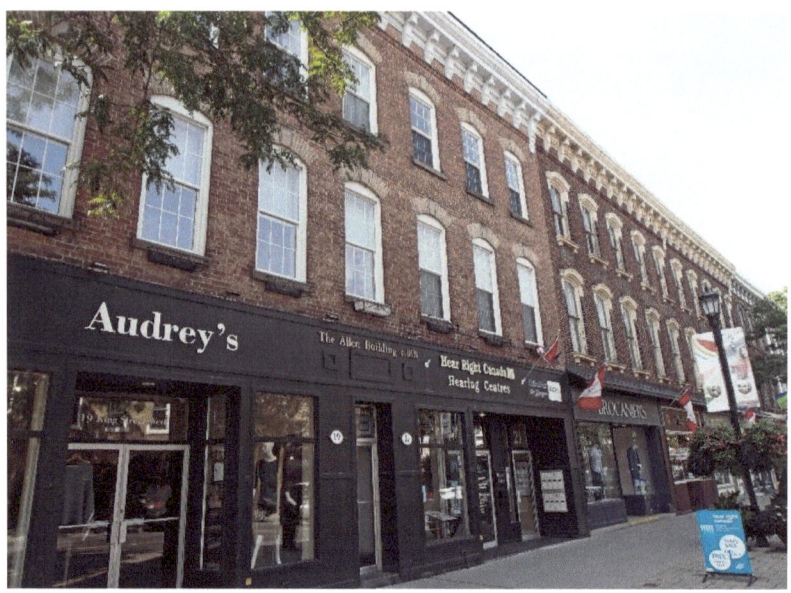

19-23 King Street West – The façade is joined with the roofline by a bracketed boxed cornice; molded wooden trim over the segmented windows, decorated cement lugsills under the windows.

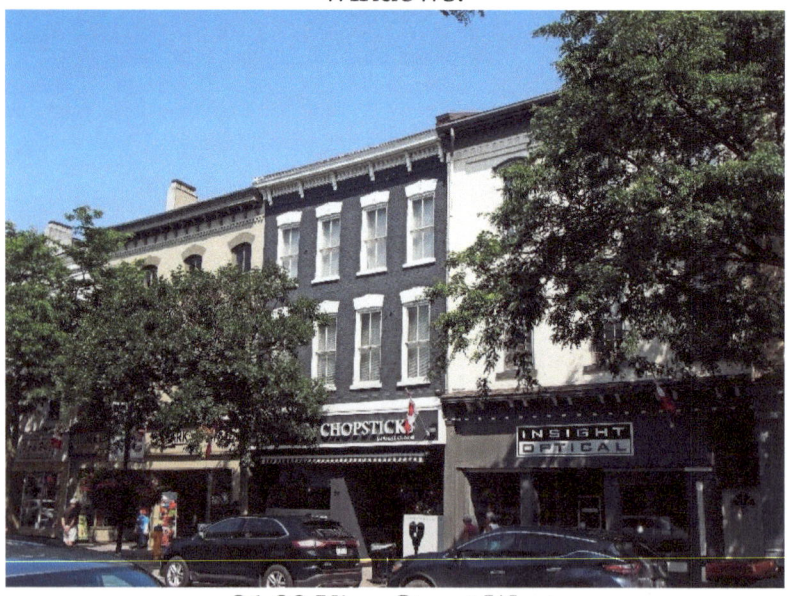

24-30 King Street West

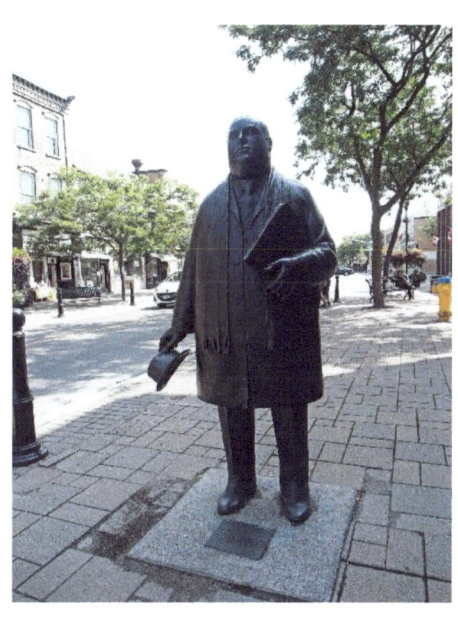

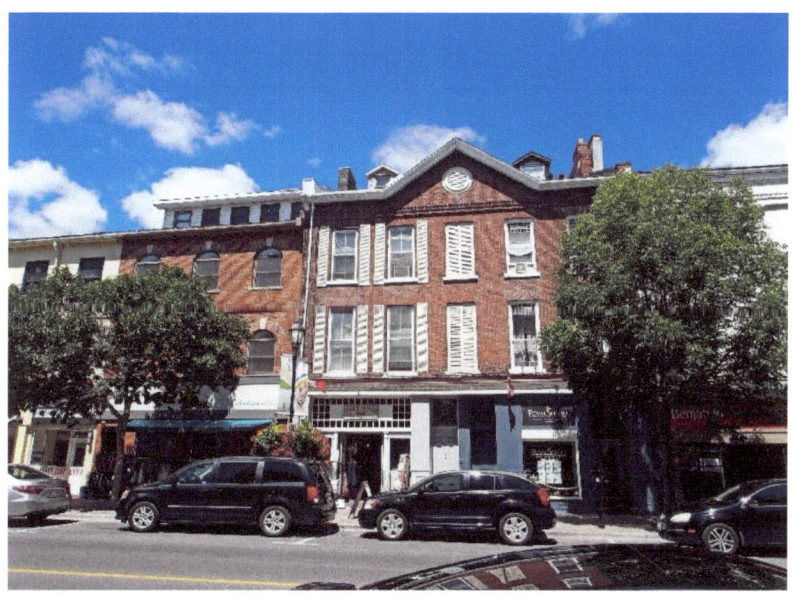

34-40 King Street West

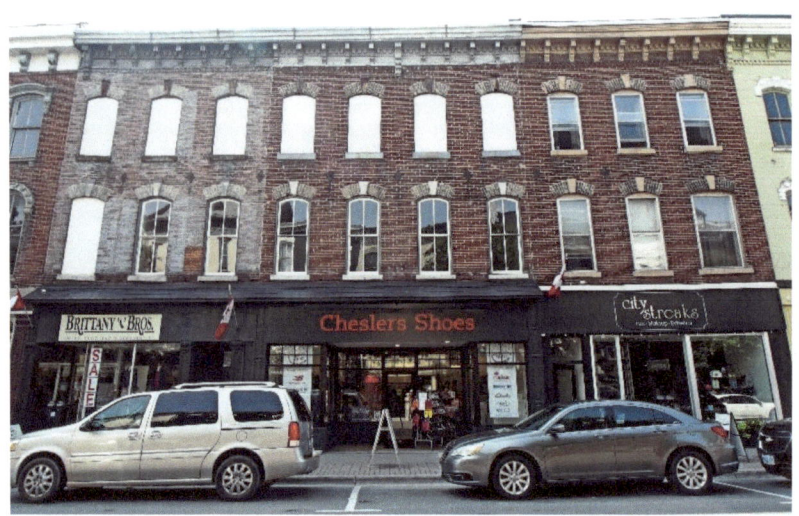

35-39 King Street West

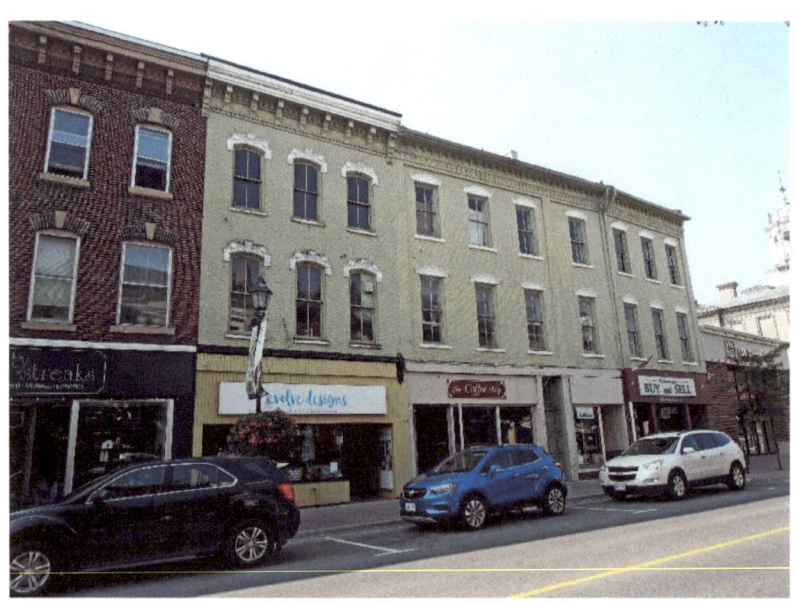

41 King Street West

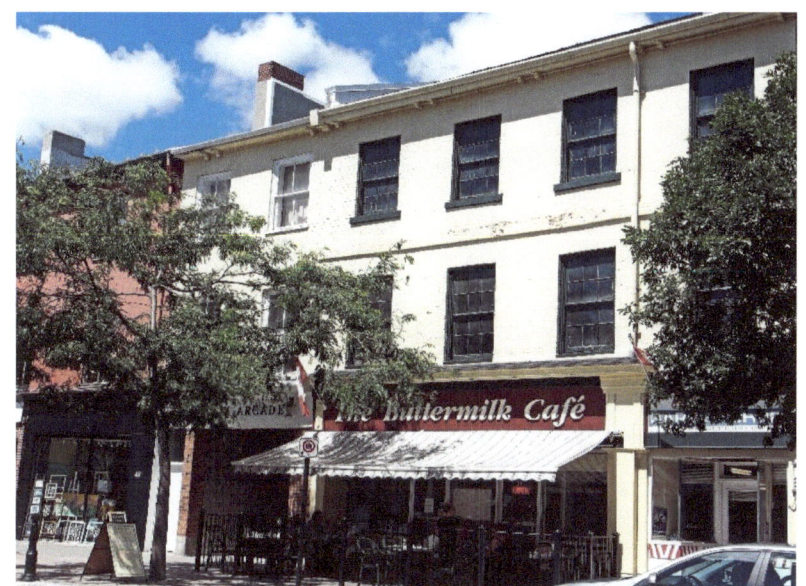

44 King Street West

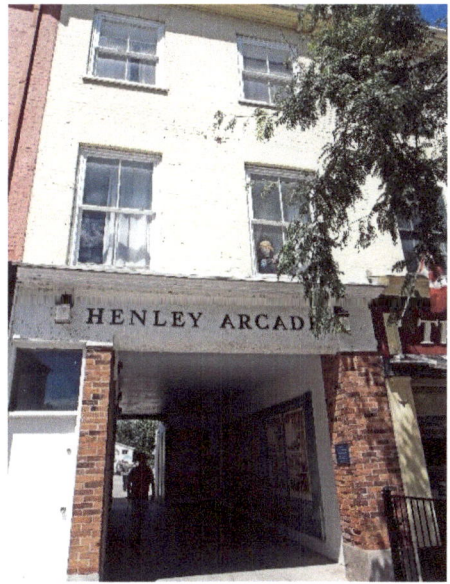

Henley Arcade

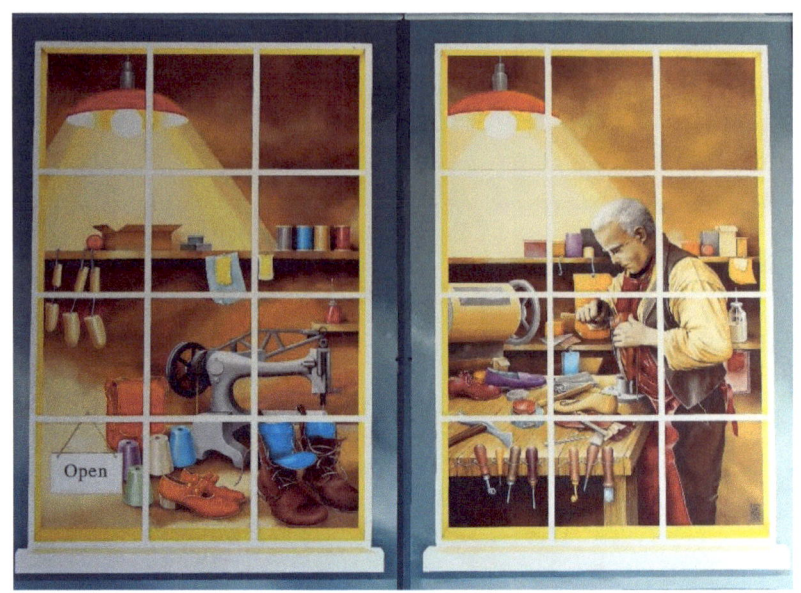

John Henley Shoe Repairs & Bicycles – 1926-1972 - murals

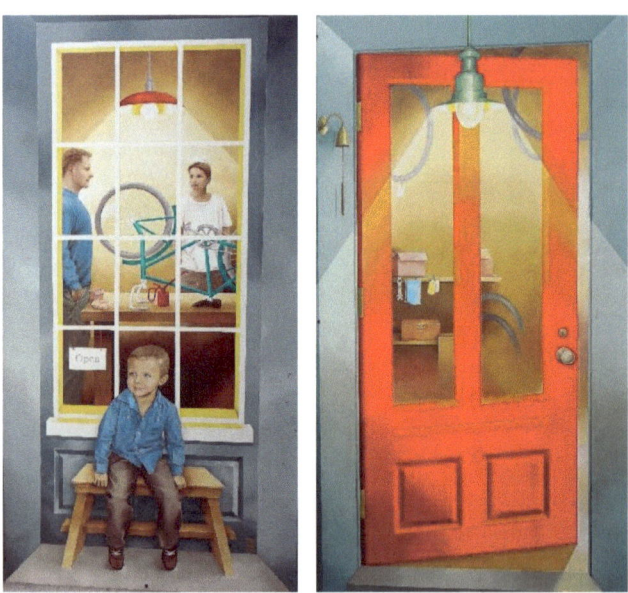

Murals by Heather Cooper

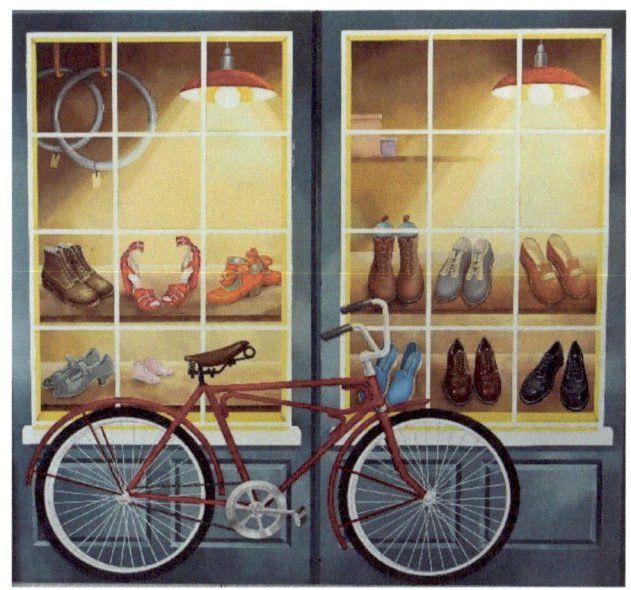

Four Seasons at the Cobourg Waterfront

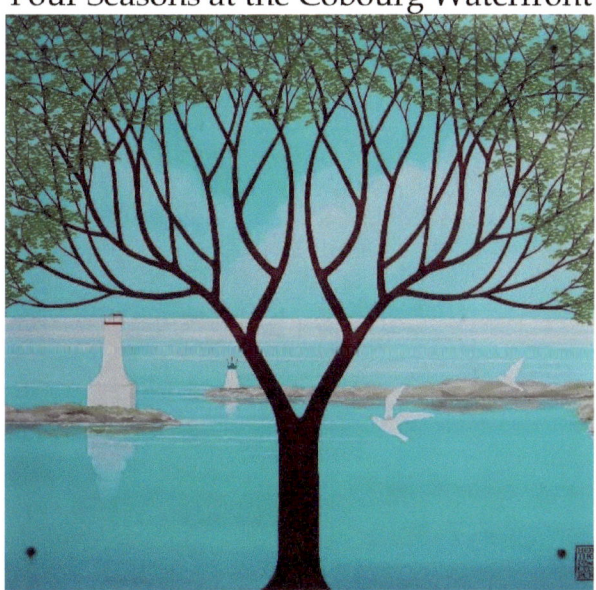

Spring
Murals by Heather Cooper

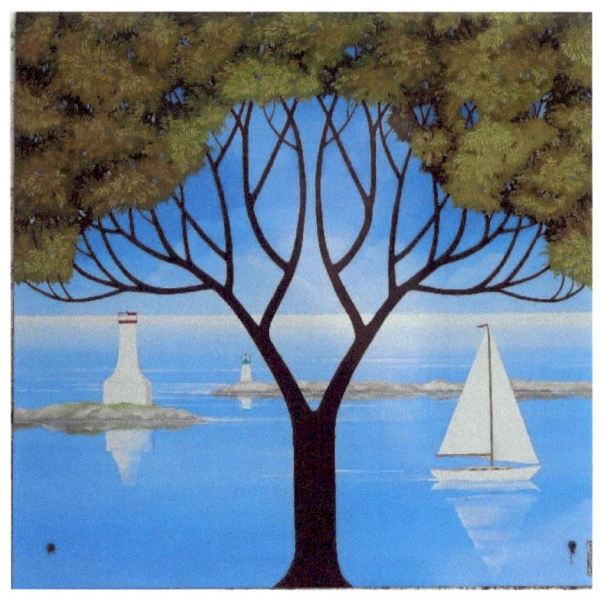

Summer

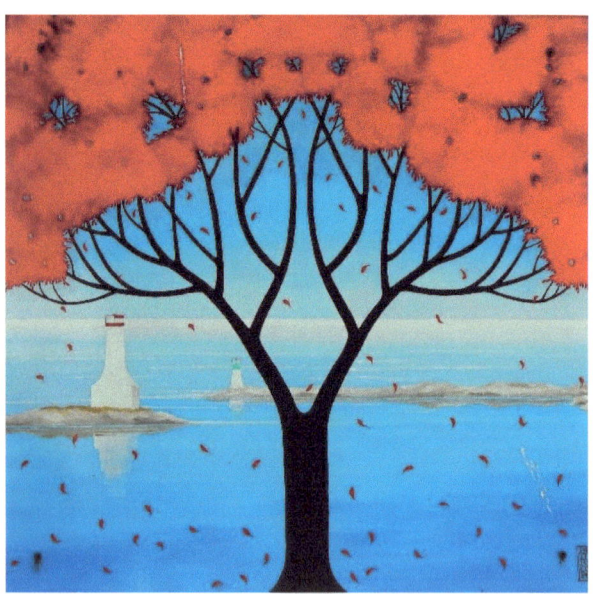

Fall

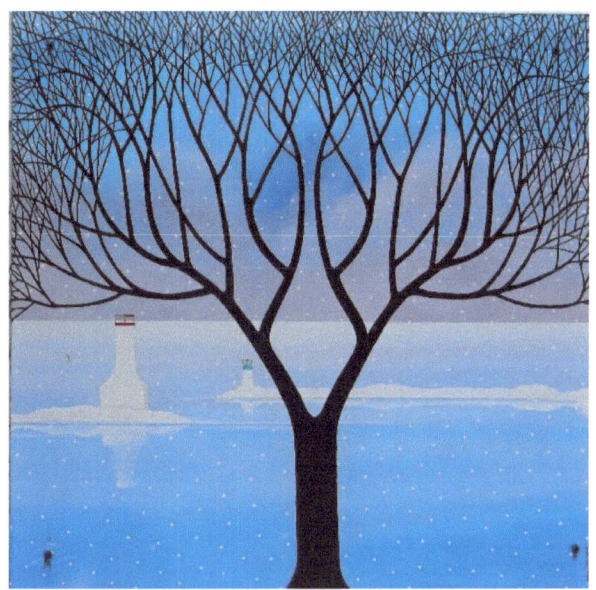

Winter

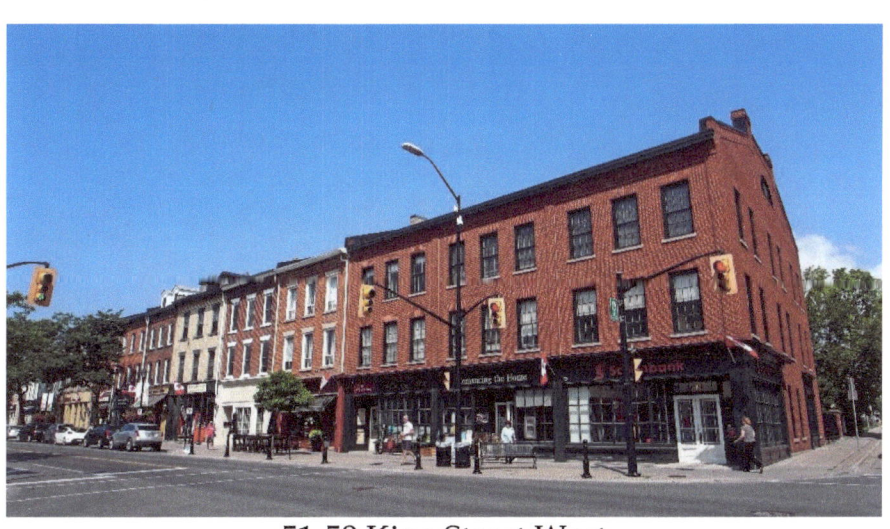

51-59 King Street West

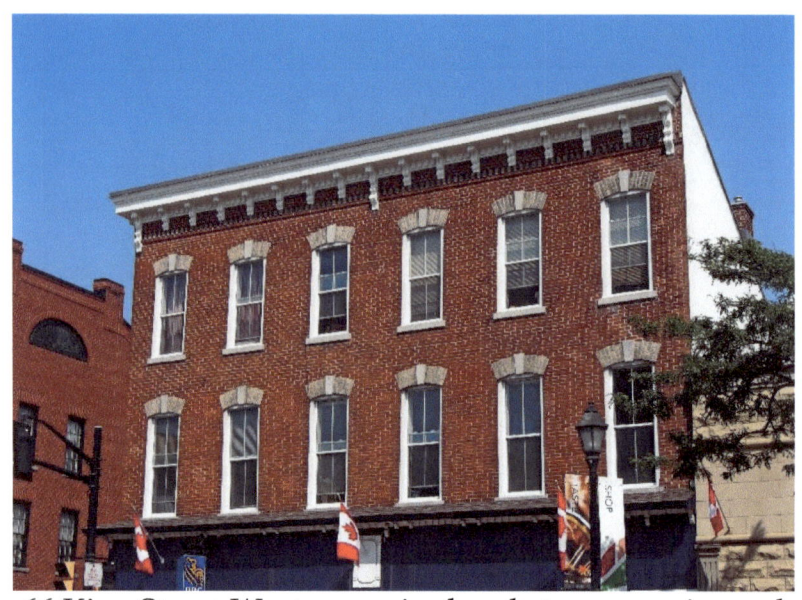

66 King Street West – cornice brackets, voussoirs and keystones over windows

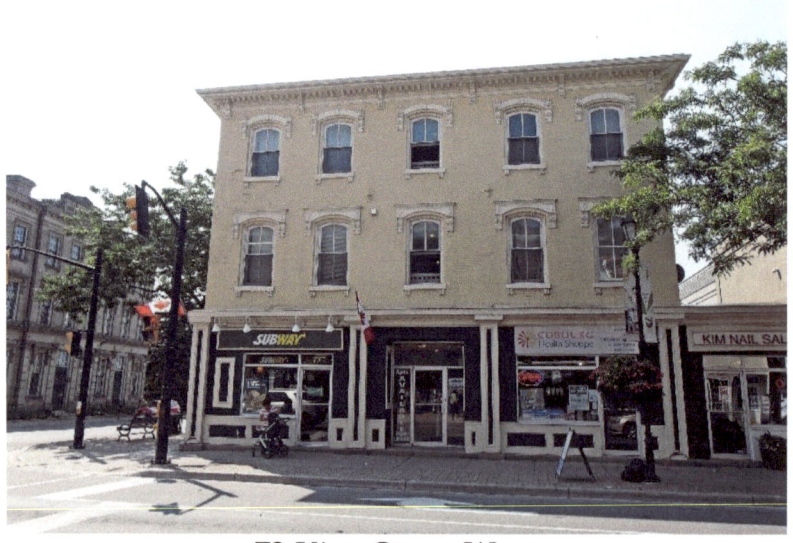

73 King Street West

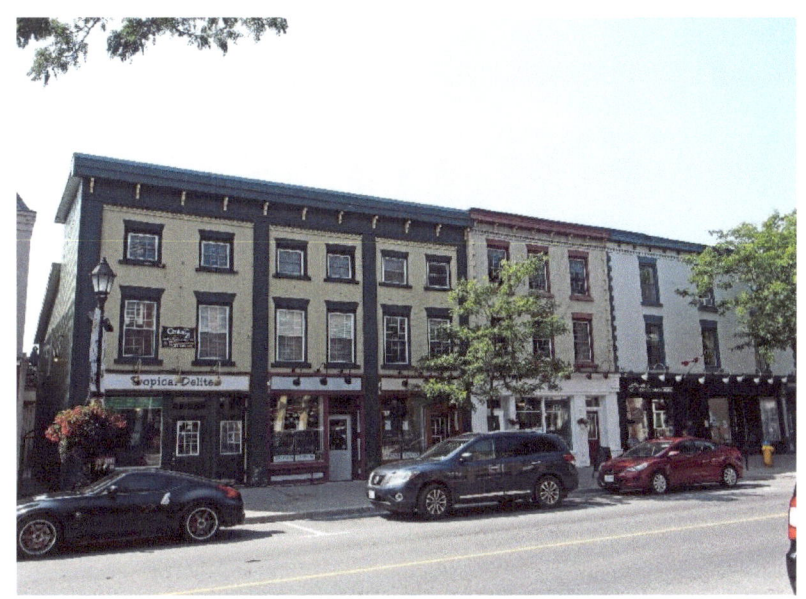

79-91 King Street West

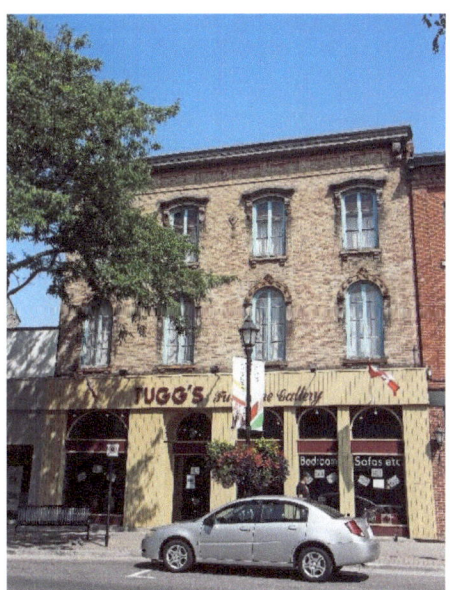

86 King Street West

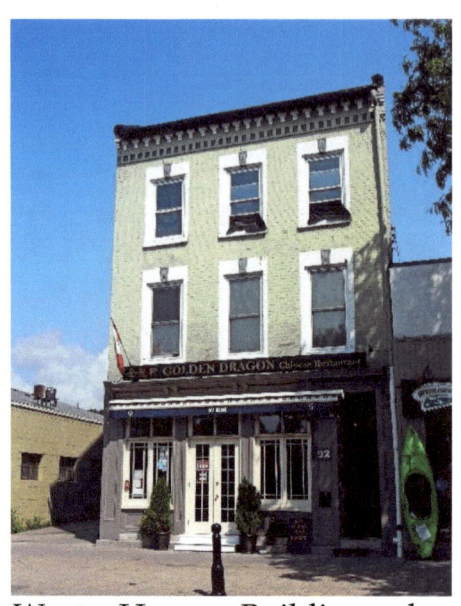

92 King Street West – Heenan Building – decorative cornice

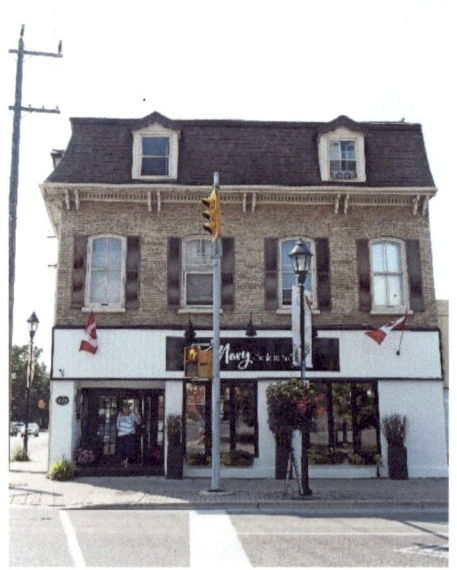

123 King Street West

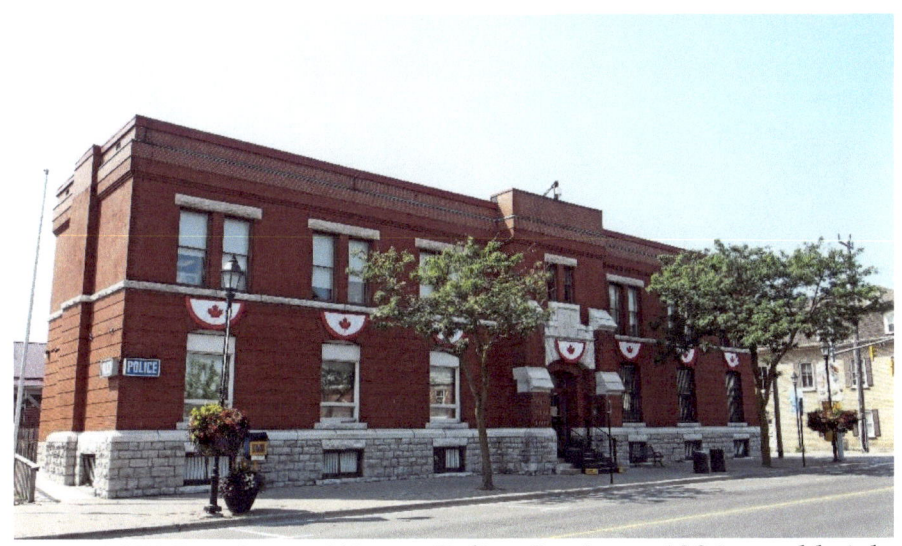

107 King Street West – Police Station – 1904 – red brick laid in stretcher bond, projected limestone foundation, lugsills, lintels, quoins on the buttressed entrance

This imposing red-brick and stone building once housed the 40th Northumberland Regiment and the Canadian Garrison Artillery and was a recruitment center in two world wars. The letters E.R. on the keystone over the doorway stand for Edwardus Rex since it was built in 1904 during the reign of Edward VII. Thousands of soldiers passed through here during World War I and a large part of the building was converted to dormitories. The large drill hall was the scene of Saturday night dances which were popular with the young women of Cobourg. It was also later used for community events such as the annual Motor Show. In 1968 the building was sold and became the town's main police station.

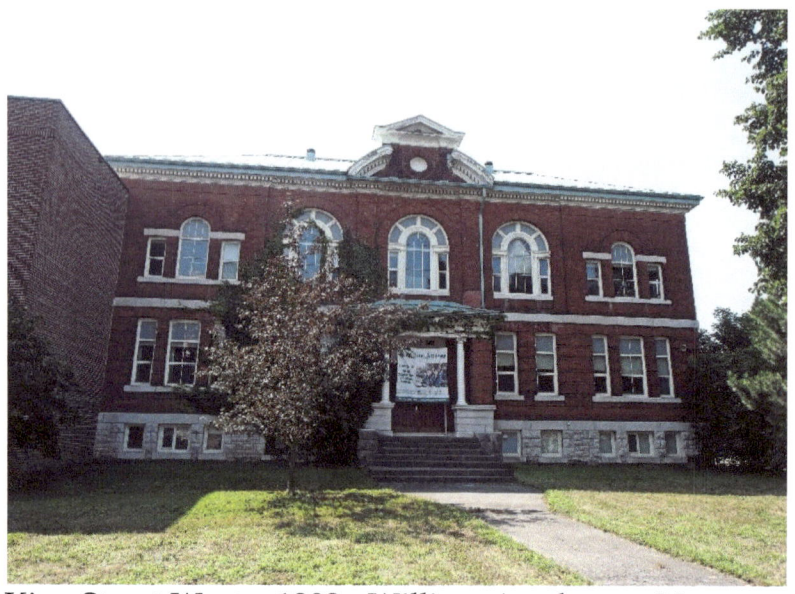

135 King Street West – 1902 - William Academy - Now a private school, this building was formerly the home of Cobourg Collegiate. Many men from the town who served in WW1 attended high school here and some of them returned to finish their studies after their time at the front. Built in 1902 in a style known as Edwardian Classical, the building features oversized Palladian windows on the second level which add drama to its front façade. Additions to the school building were made in 1939 and during the 1960s, but in 2015 the collegiate moved to a new facility on King Street East.

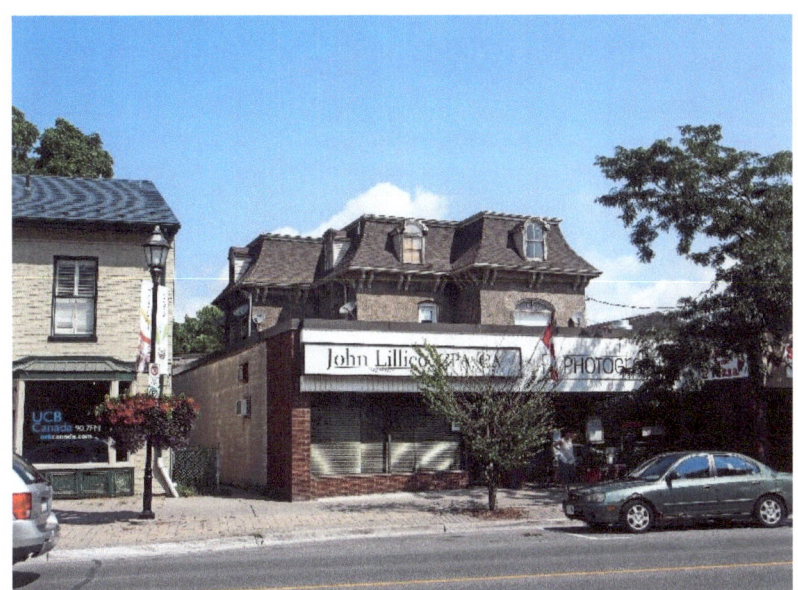

144 King Street West - The Second Empire-style home behind the Shawarma House was built in 1874 by William Battell, a local builder who later became a mayor of Cobourg. It once had stables, a coach house and an elaborate fence in front. William Beattie, the minister of St. Andrew's Presbyterian Church, was a lodger here and purchased the house after Battell's death. When war broke out in 1914, Beattie enlisted as a chaplain of the 40th Regiment of the Cobourg Battalion and rose to become the chaplain of the entire 2nd Division. His letters from the front sent to the local newspapers comprise a remarkable chronicle of the war. In describing his first impression of the Western Front, he wrote: "Imagine trying to live for over a year in the trenches which you have seen workmen in Cobourg digging when laying sewers." After the war, Beattie moved to Ottawa and in 1956 the house was converted to a Canadian Tire store and the front addition has been a retail space ever since.

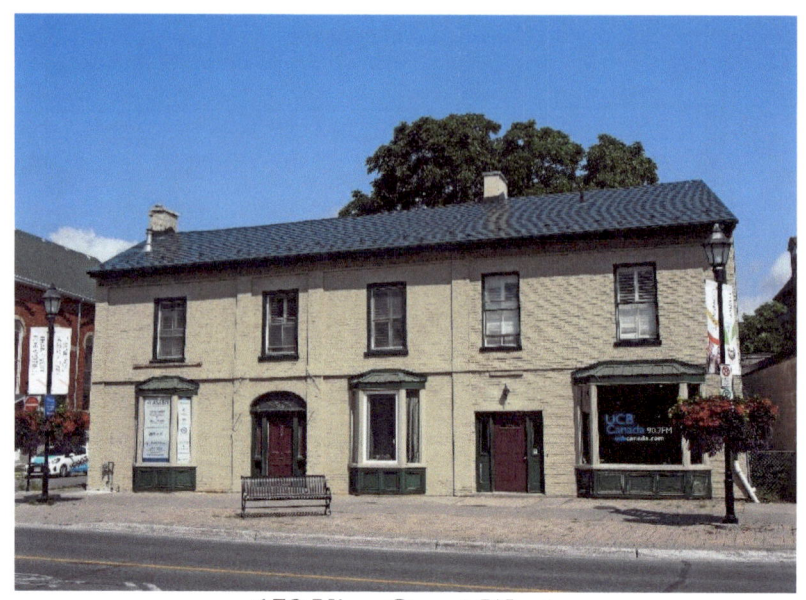

150 King Street West

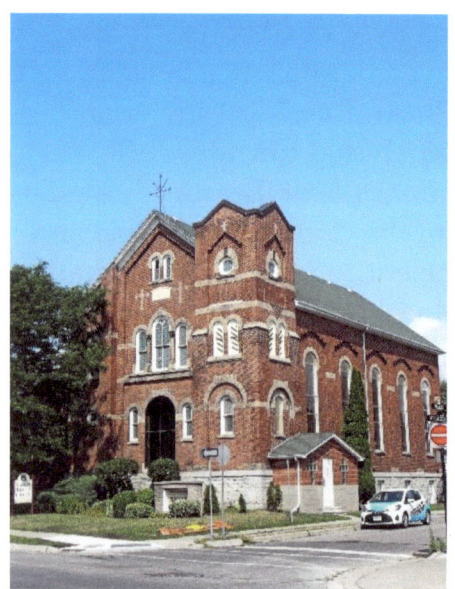

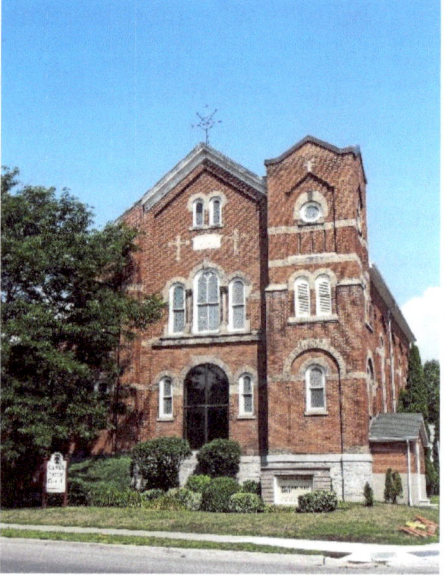

166 King Street West – Calvary Baptist Church – 1879
(Methodist Episcopal Church) – Romanesque Revival style –
banding, voussoirs and keystones, patterned brickwork

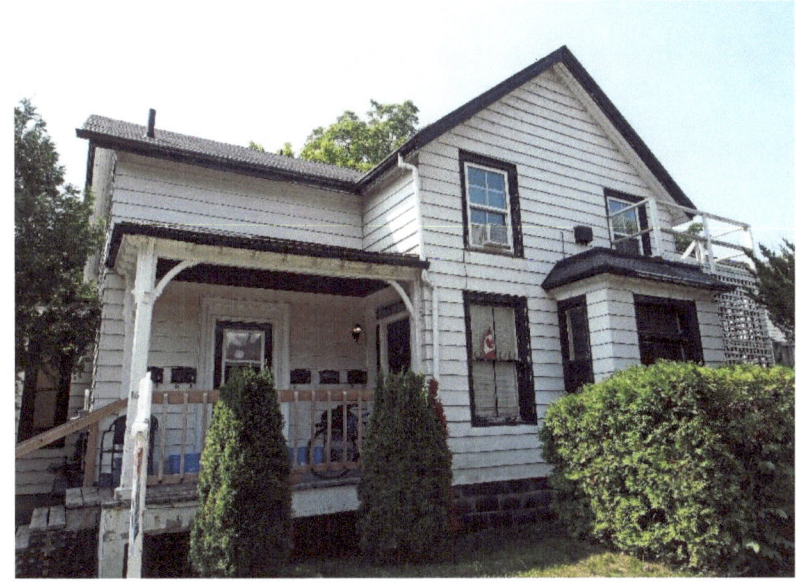

16_ King Street West

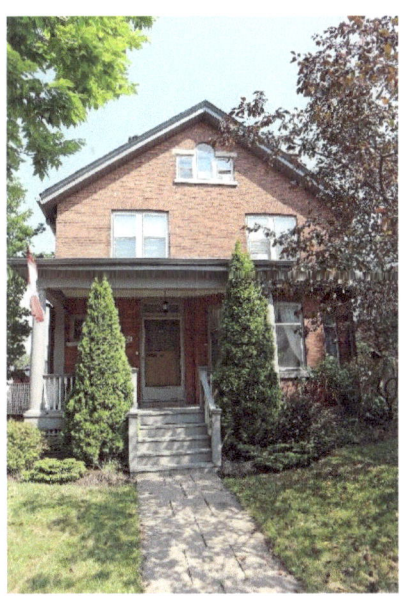

170 King Street West

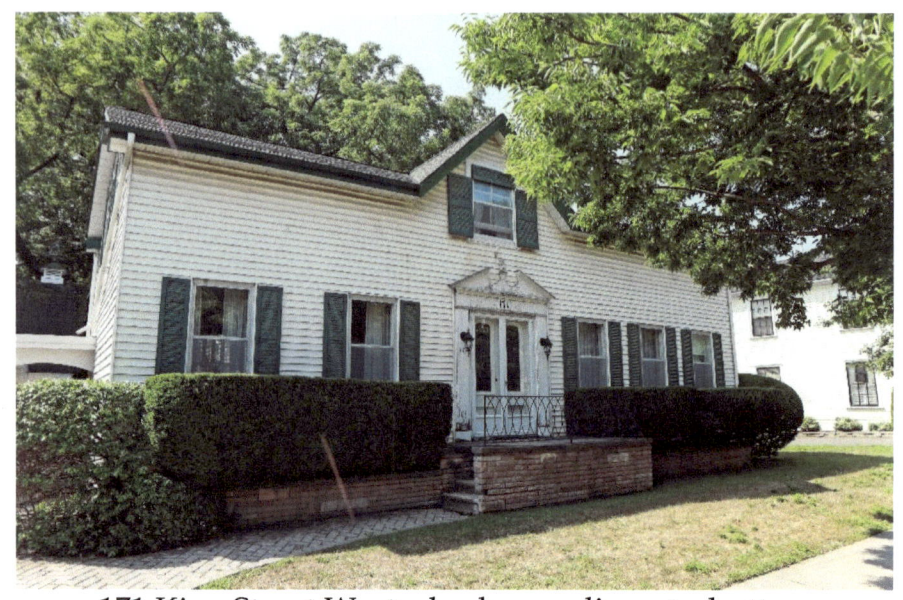

171 King Street West – broken pediment, shutters

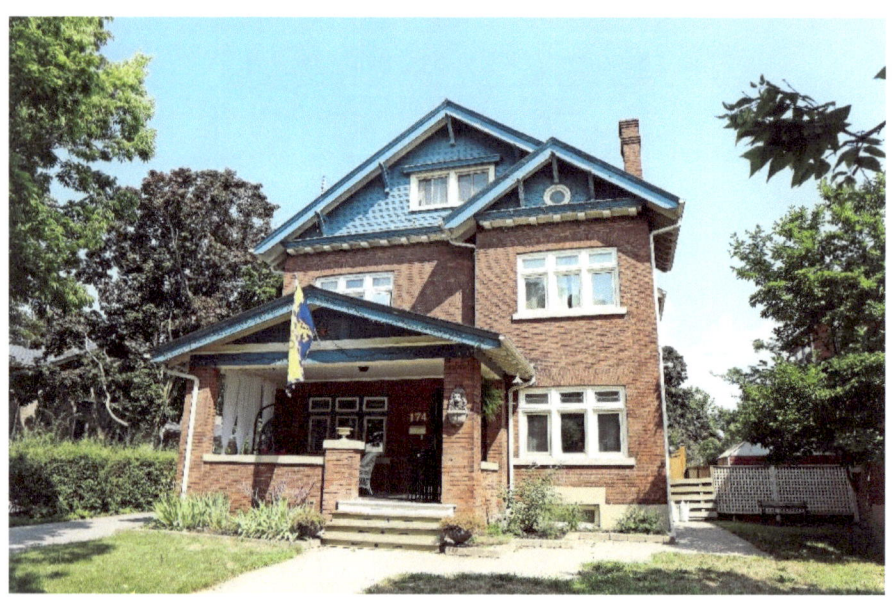

174 King Street West

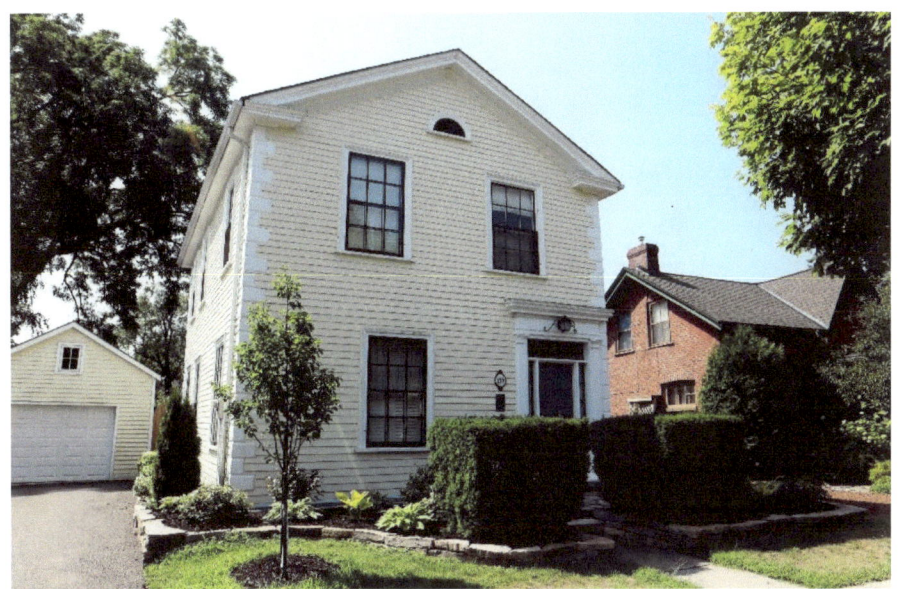

177 King Street West - c. 1848 - Greek revival style town house with exterior corner blocks of wood dressed to resemble stone, cornice return on gable, sidelights and transom, engaged columns

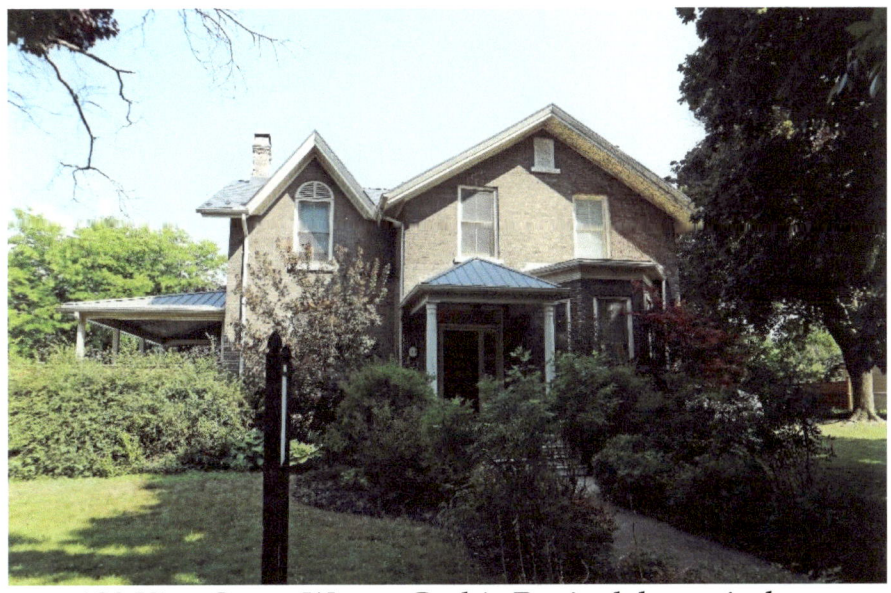

180 King Street West – Gothic Revival, bay window

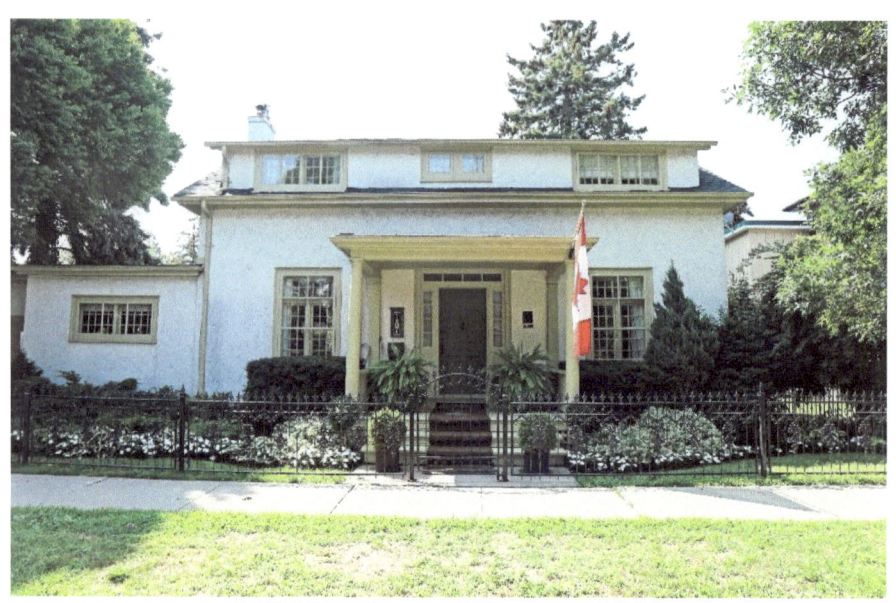

187 King Street West – c. 1840

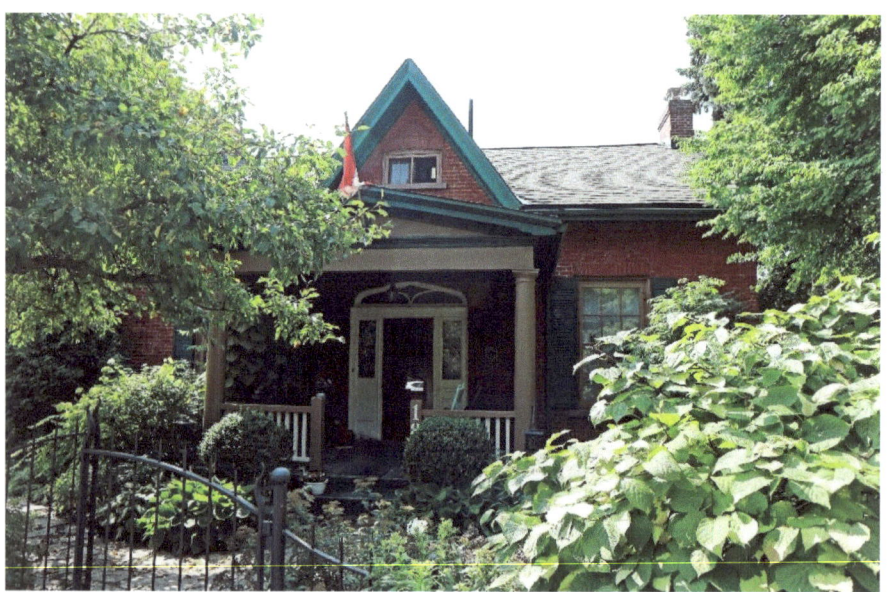

189 King Street West – c. 1852

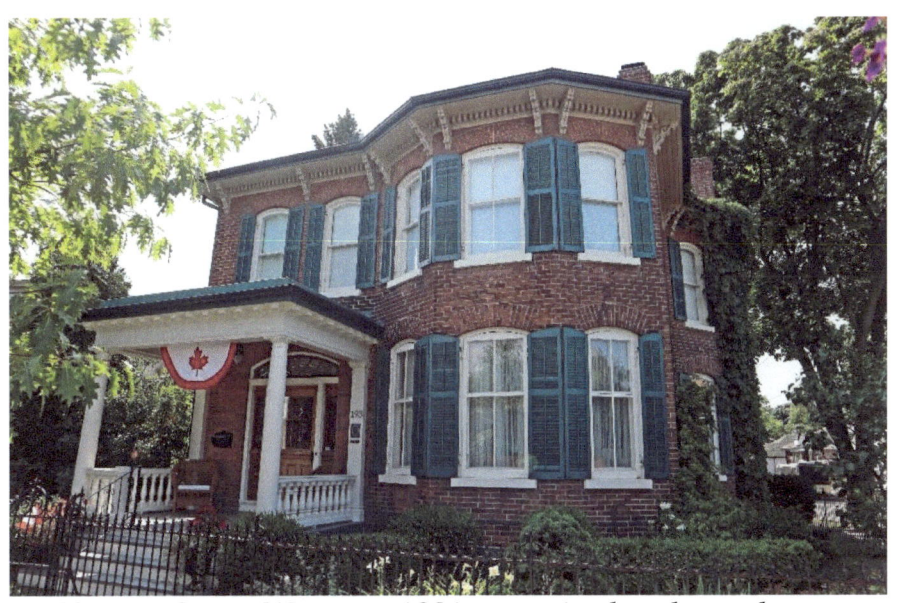

193 King Street West – c. 1891 – cornice brackets, shutters

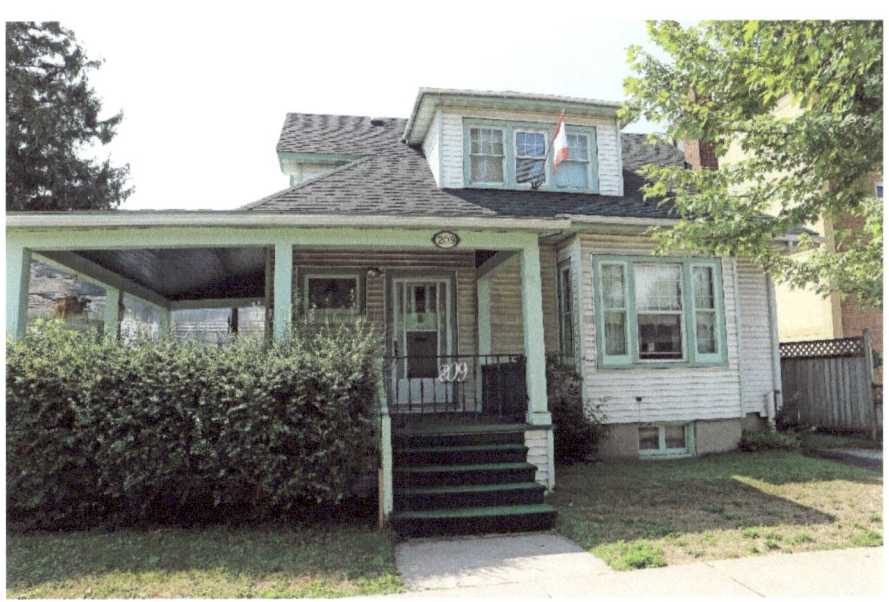

209 King Street West

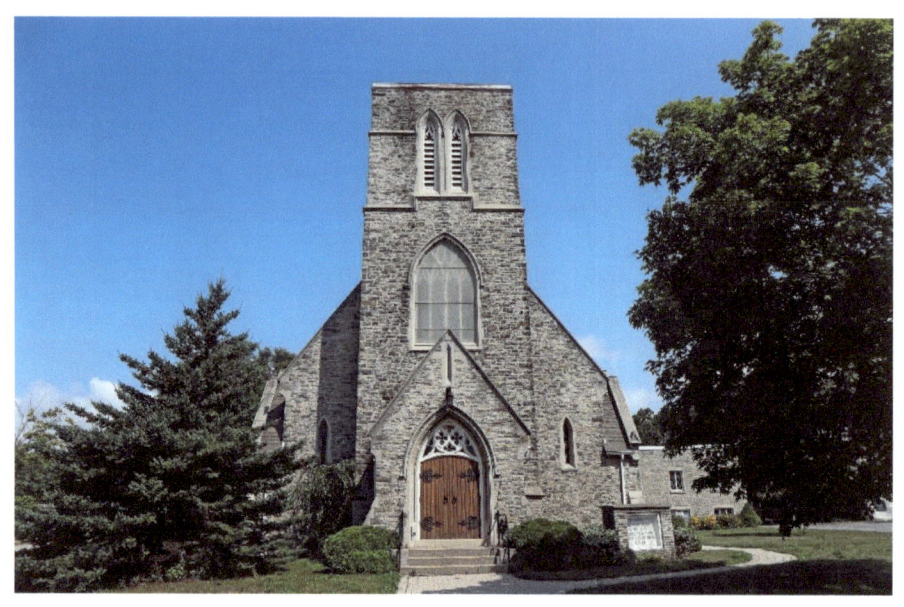

200 King Street West – St. Andrew's Presbyterian Church –
Gothic Revival style – lancet windows, buttresses

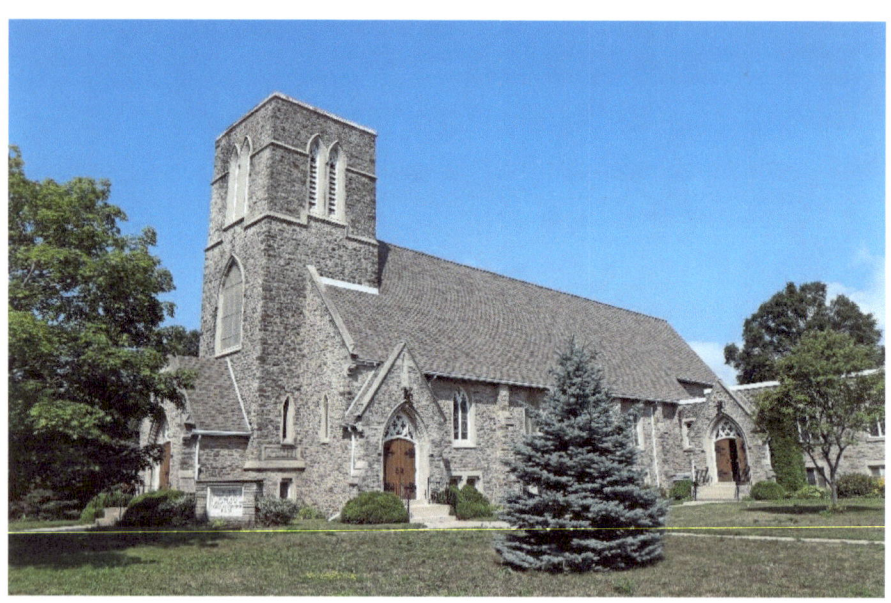

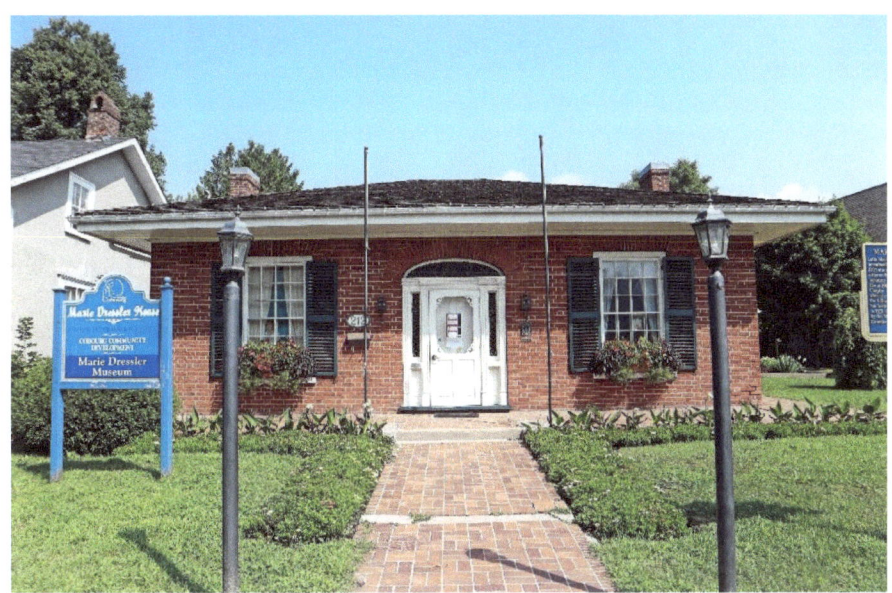

212 King Street West – This Ontario cottage was the birthplace of Oscar-winning Hollywood actress Marie Dressler. Completely restored, it now serves as Cobourg Tourist Office. Memorabilia from Marie Dressler's career and video clips from her movies are on display.

Built in 1833, the cottage was of simple design, with two rooms off each side of a central hallway. It had embellishments suited to a family of means, such as high ceilings, large windows, impressive mouldings and an elaborate front door.

Dressler was a youngster who had a dream of being on the stage; she dared to follow that dream, and persisted in the development of her craft, through times of success and failure. At an age when most stars are long forgotten by Hollywood producers, Dressler reached the pinnacle of her career.

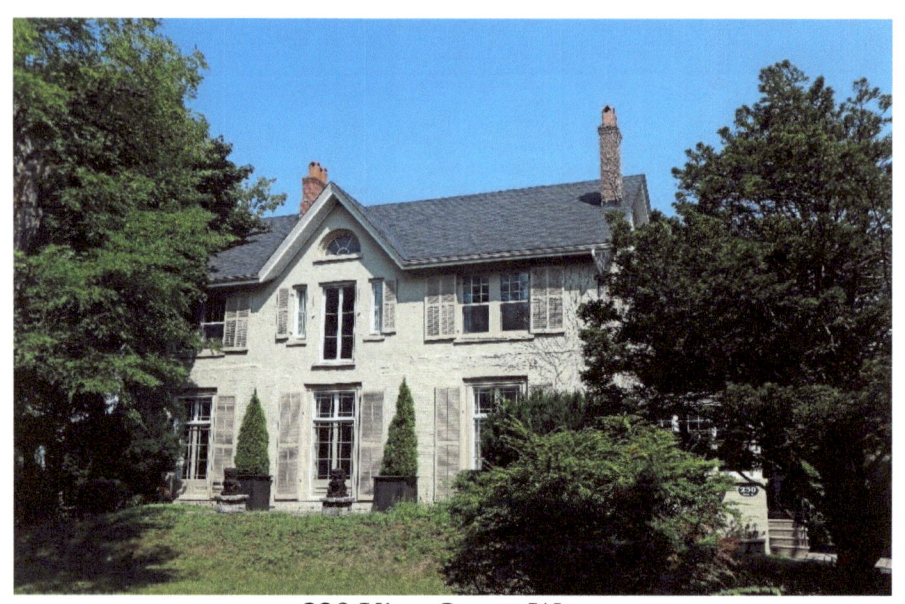

230 King Street West

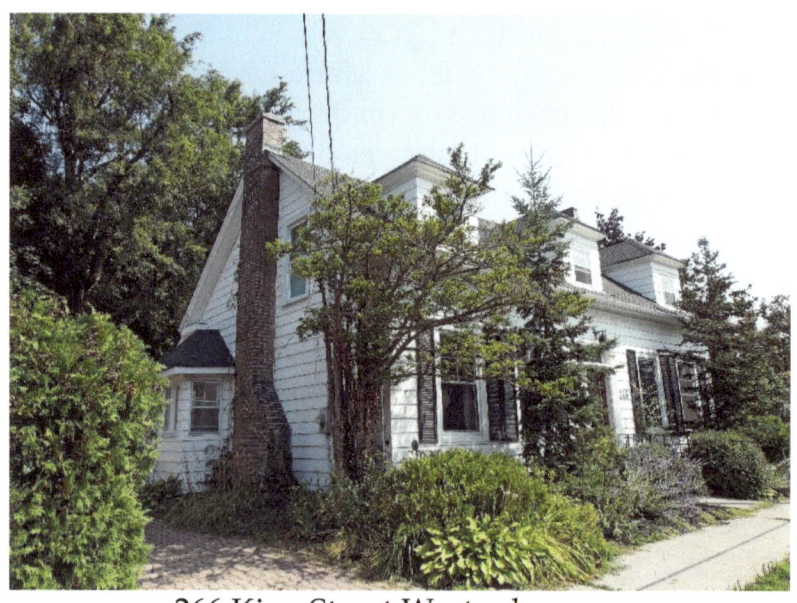

266 King Street West - dormers

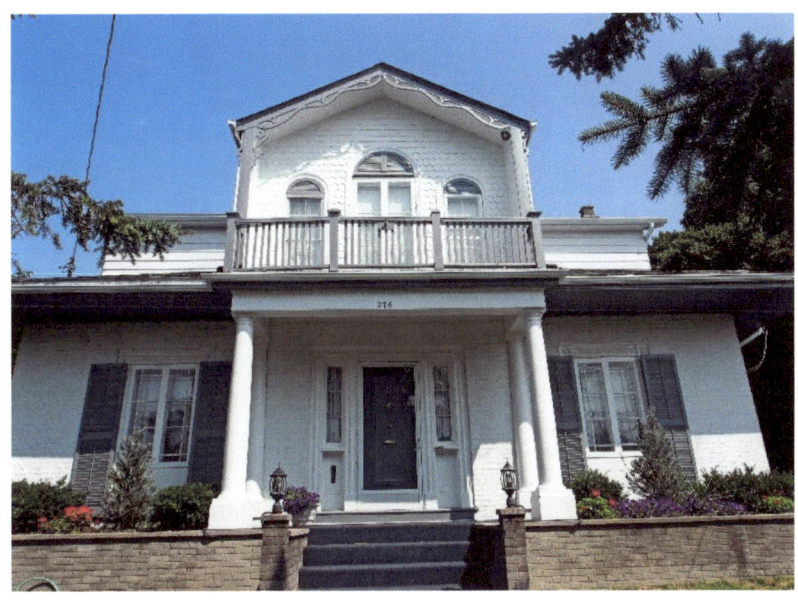

276 King Street West – second floor balcony supported by pillars, sidelights

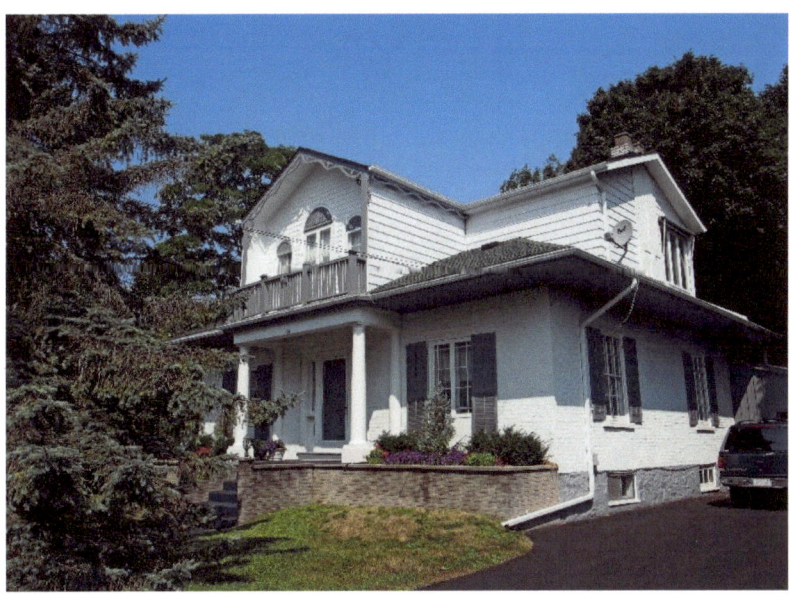

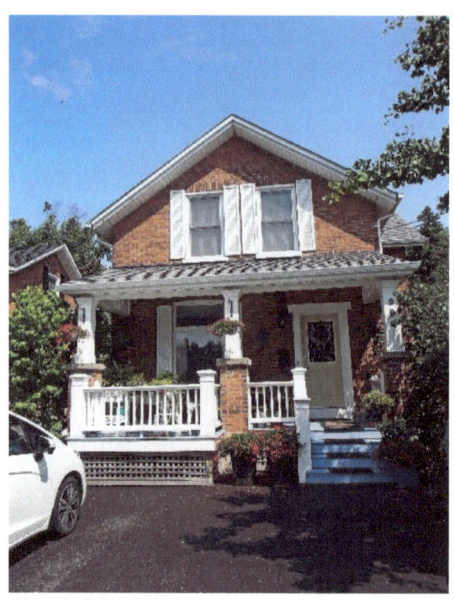

294 King Street West

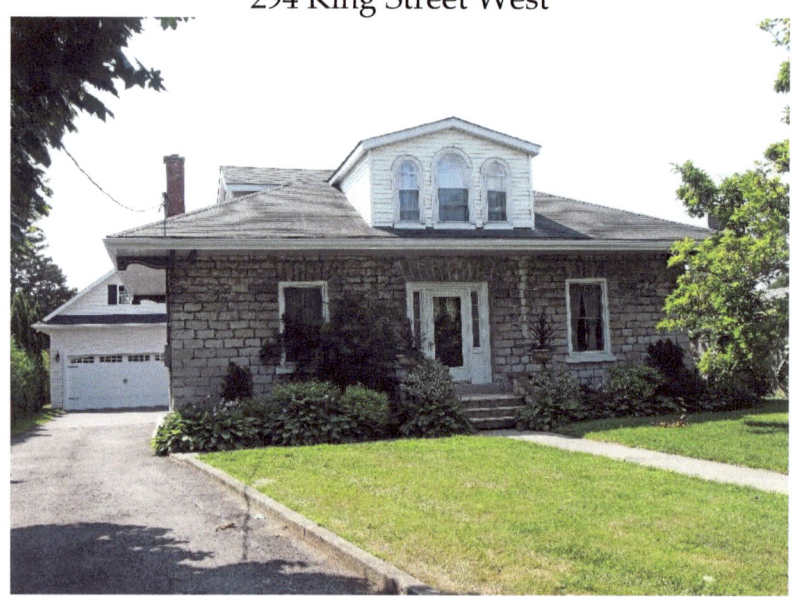

295 King Street West – c. 1847-48 – This is a Vernacular Ontario Cottage and only cut stone house in Cobourg; it was built by Alexander Sutherland and was the home of the Delanty family for many years.

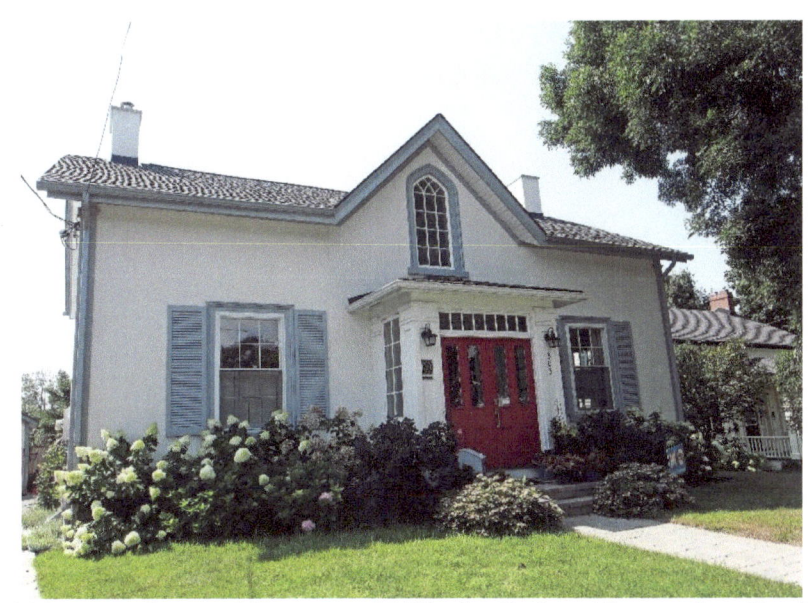

303 King Street West – c. 1850 - built by Alexander Cook

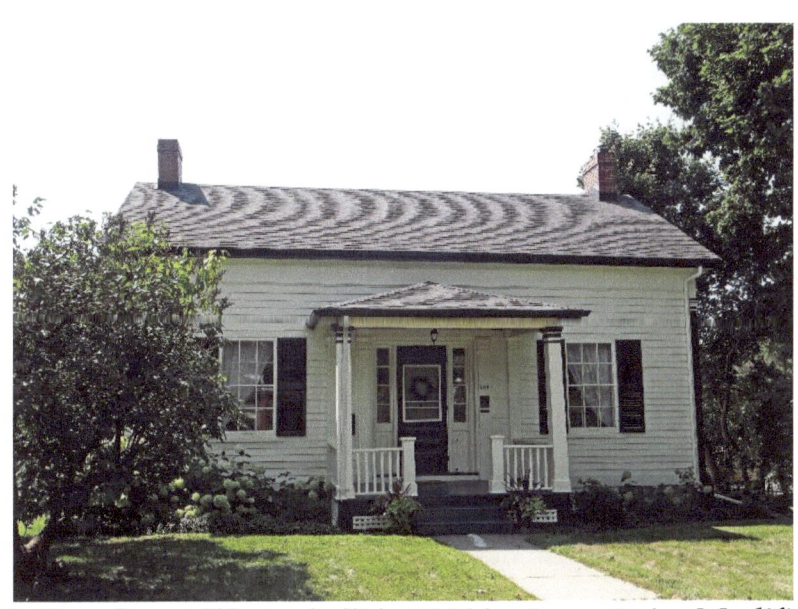

309 King Street West – built in 1854 by James Vair - Modified
Greek Revival house

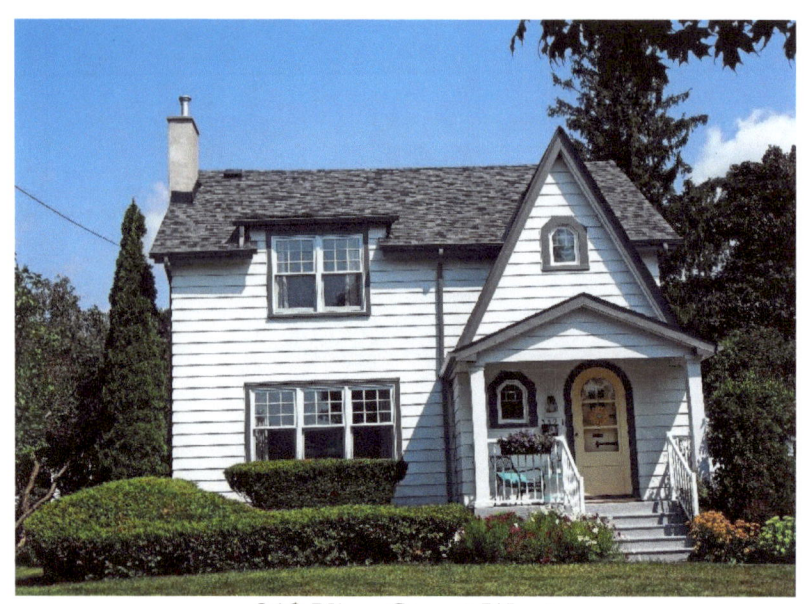

312 King Street West

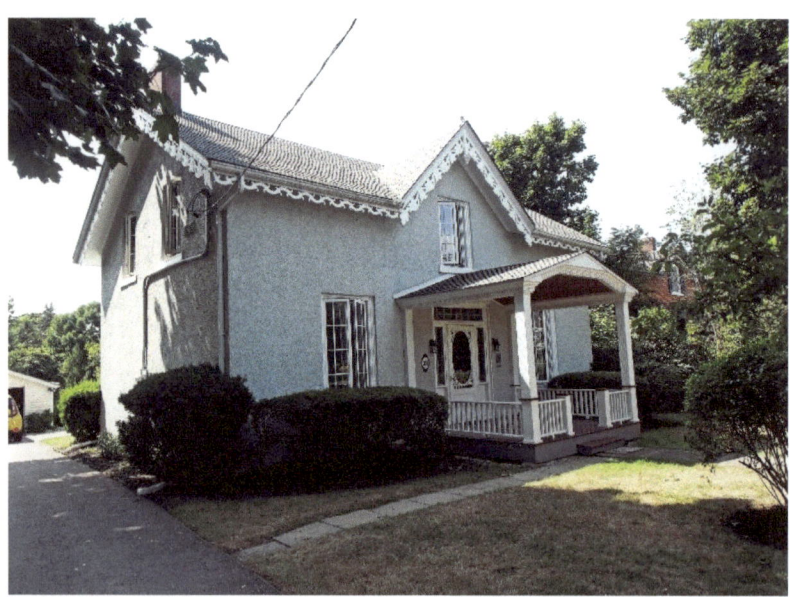

317 King Street West – c. 1850 – 1½ storey, centre hall plan, wood house sheathed in stucco, verge board trim and finial

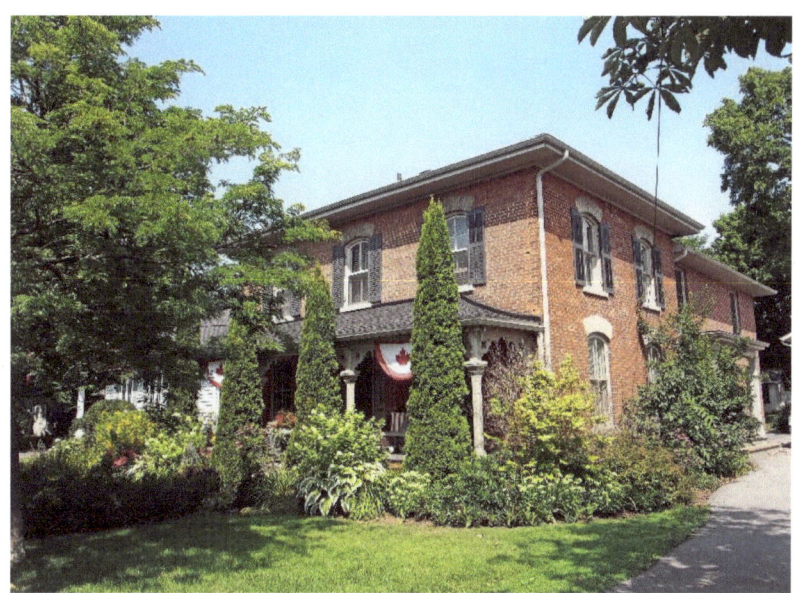

326 King Street West

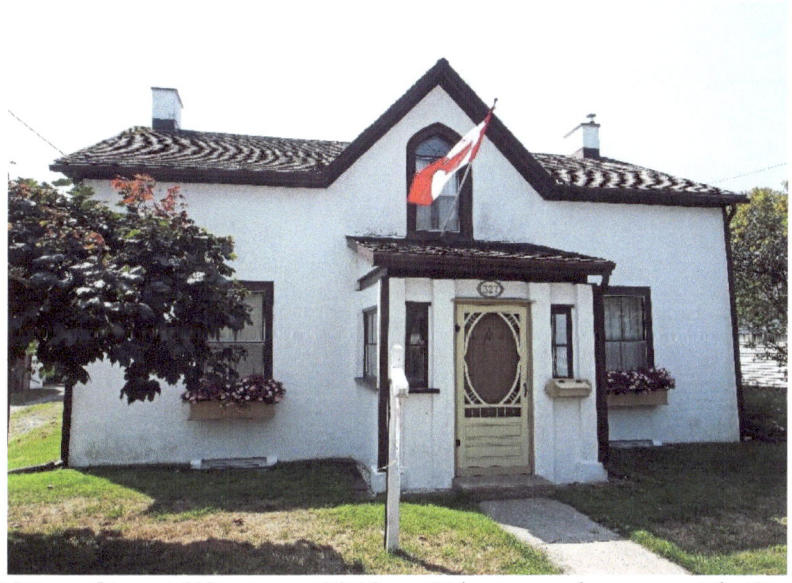

327 King Street West – c. 1840s – 1½ storey house with Gothic
Revival elements - Birthplace and boyhood home of Father
Francis P. Duffy, WWI Chaplain of the 69th New York
Regiment, Rainbow Division, U.S. Army

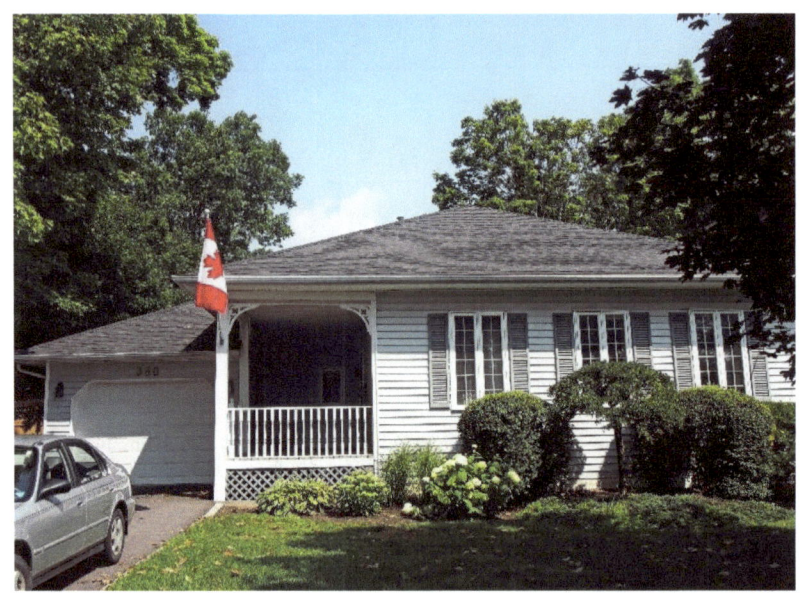

330 King Street West – hipped roof

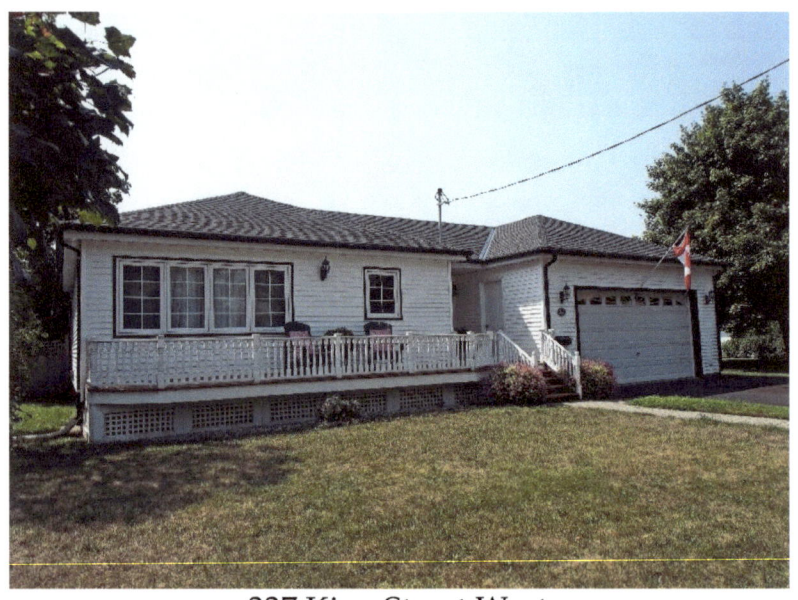

337 King Street West

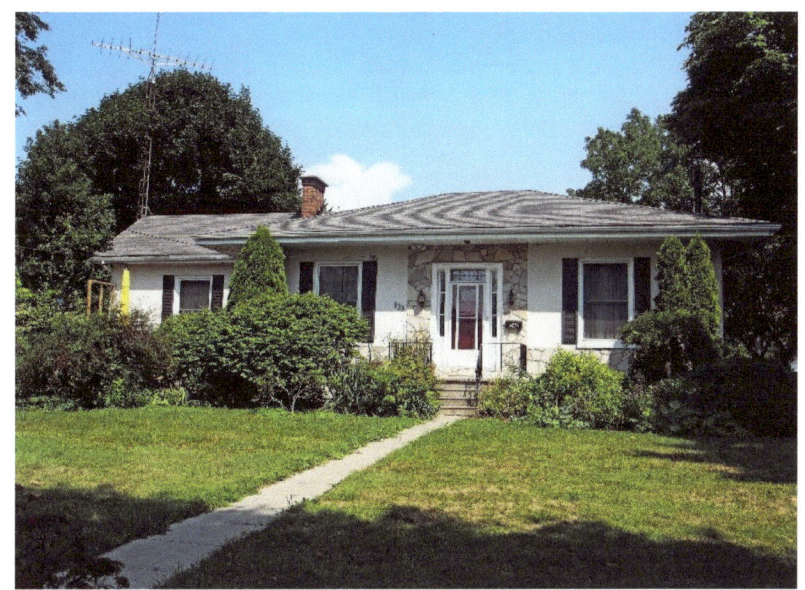

340 King Street West

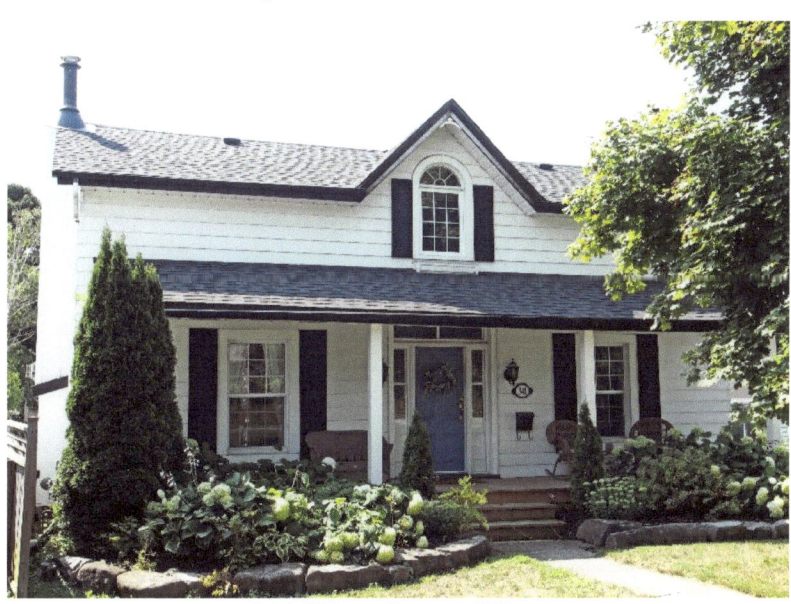

341 King Street West

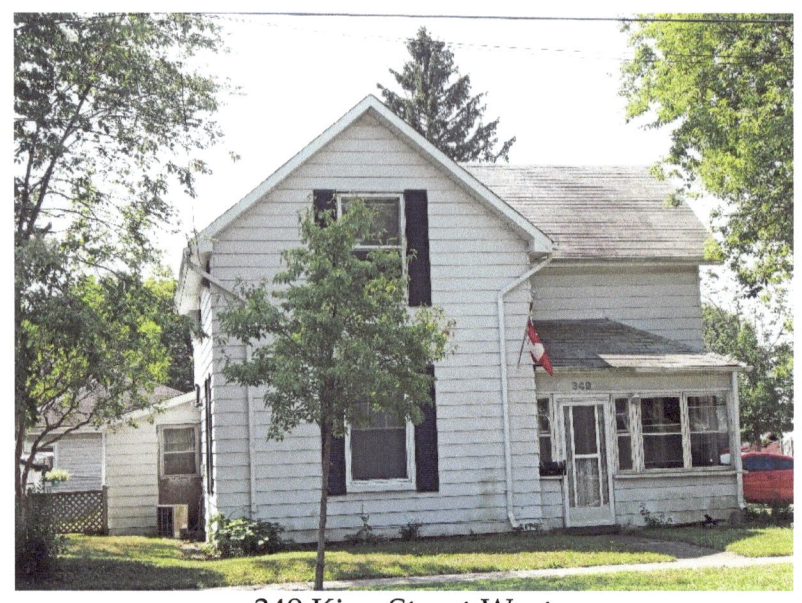

349 King Street West

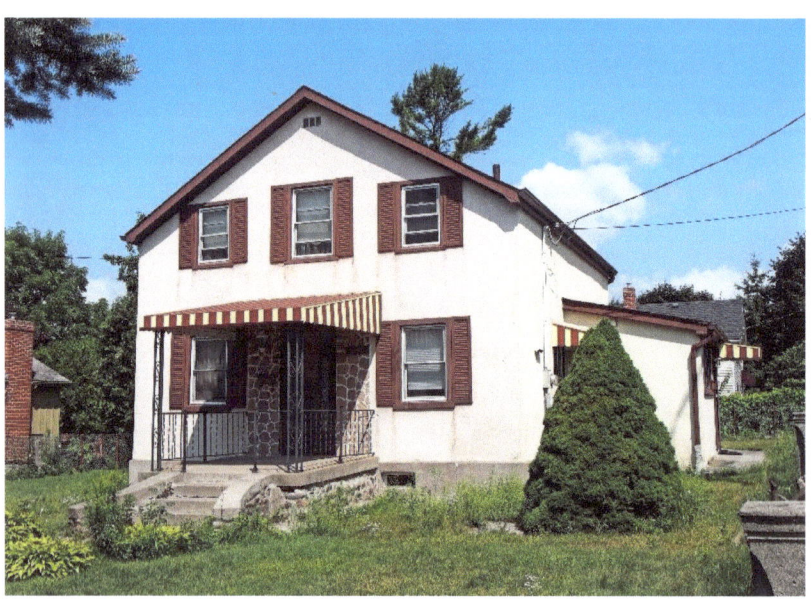

352 King Street West

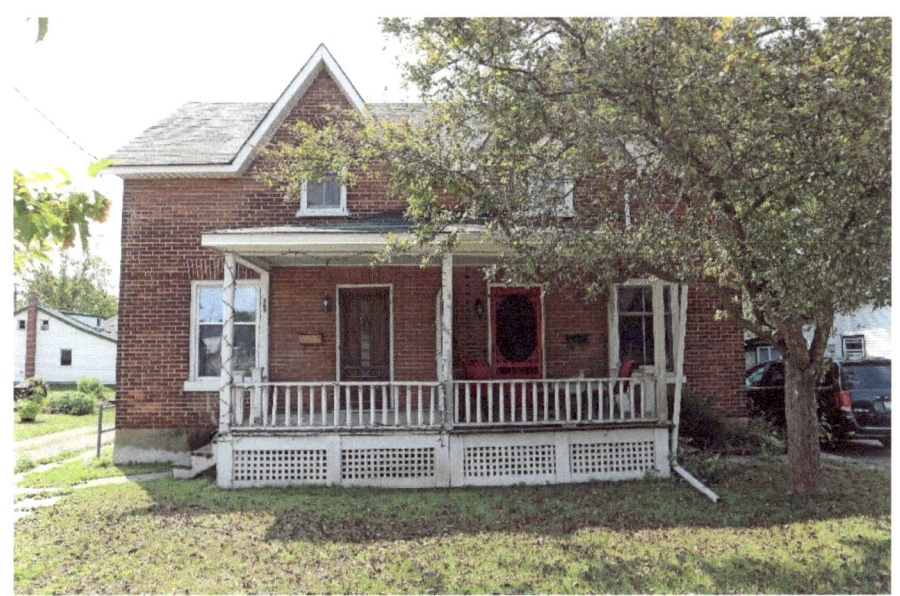

369-371 King Street West

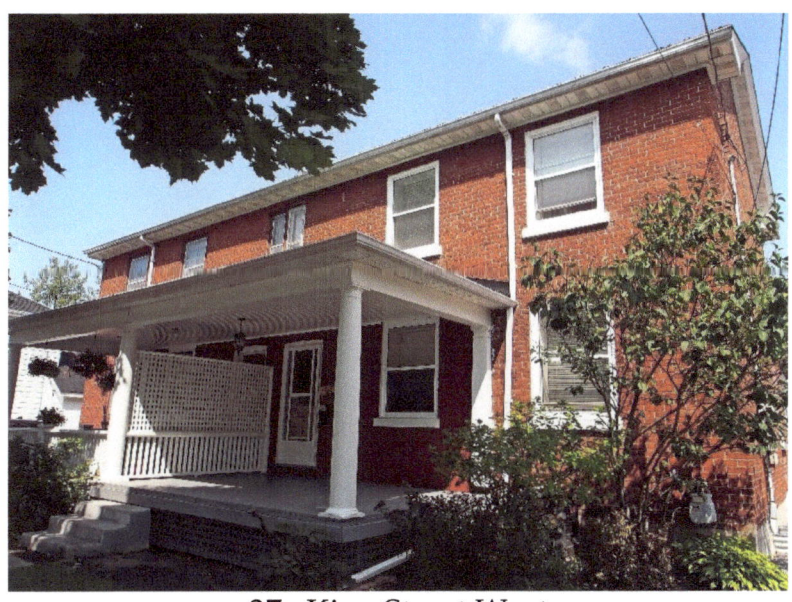

37_ King Street West

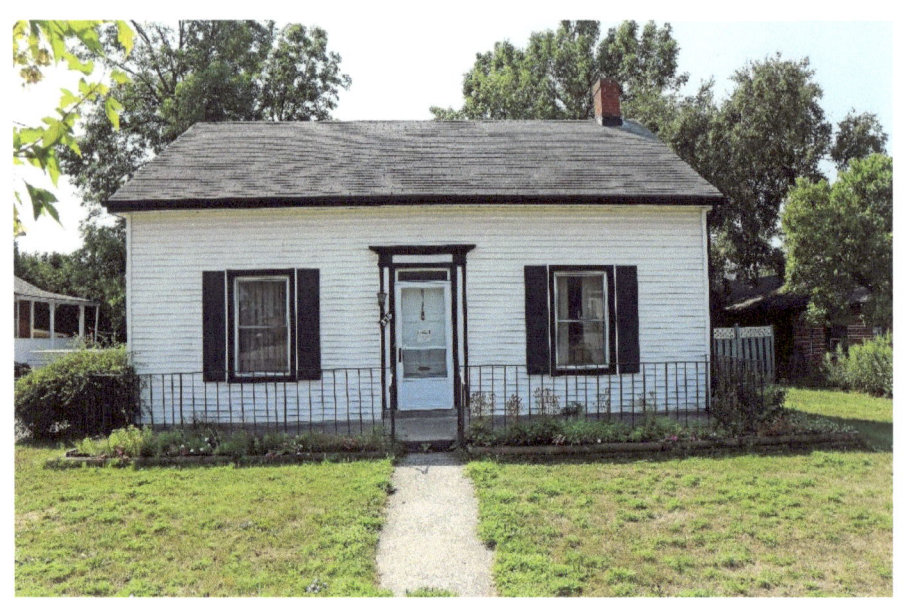

375 King Street West

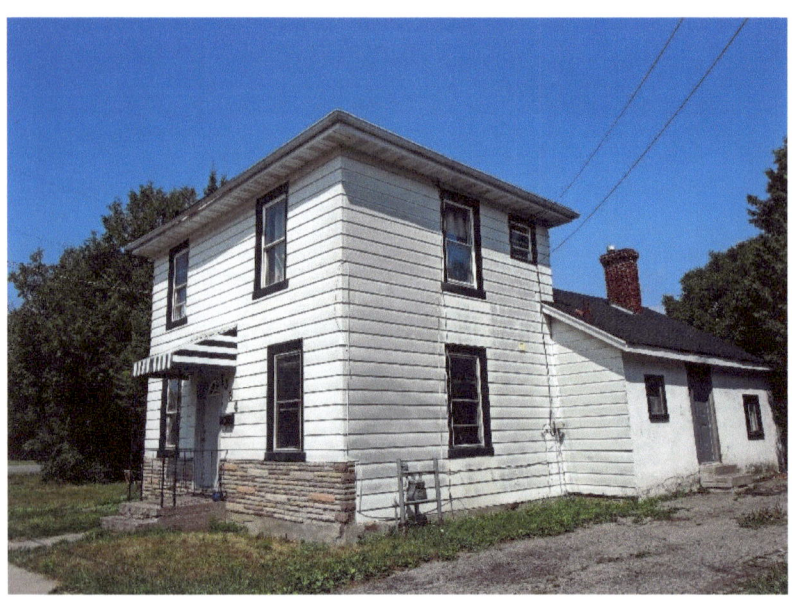

384 King Street West

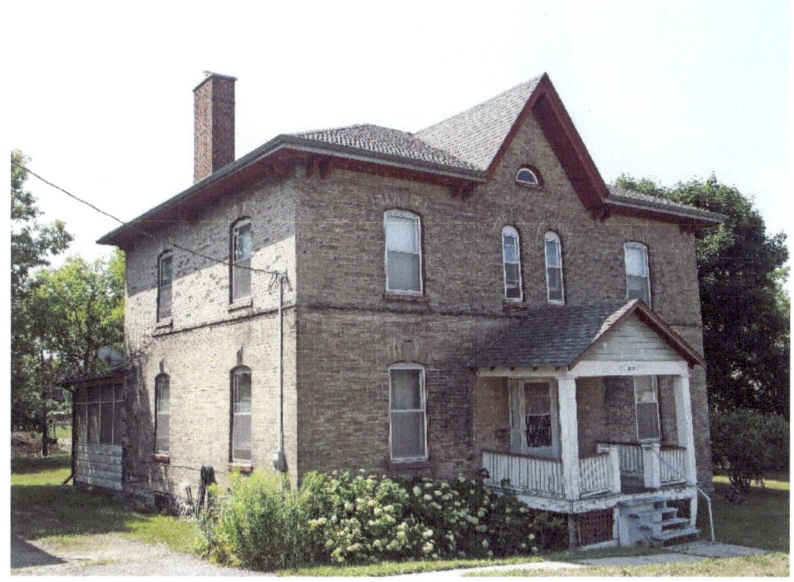

399 King Street West

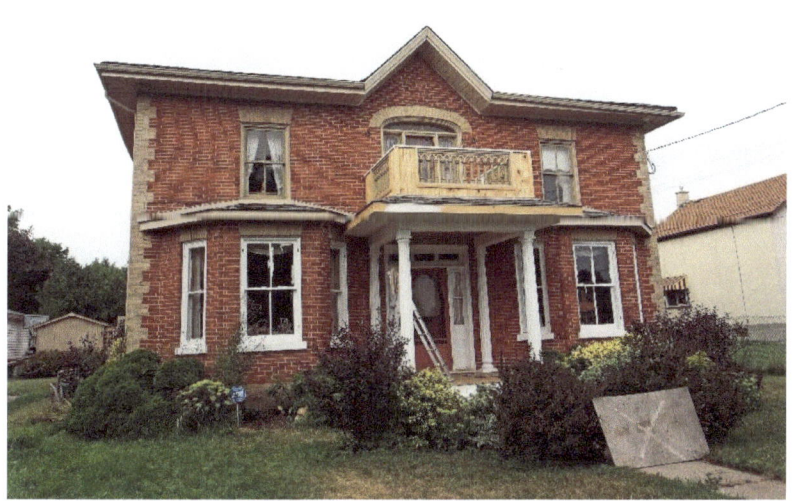

King Street West

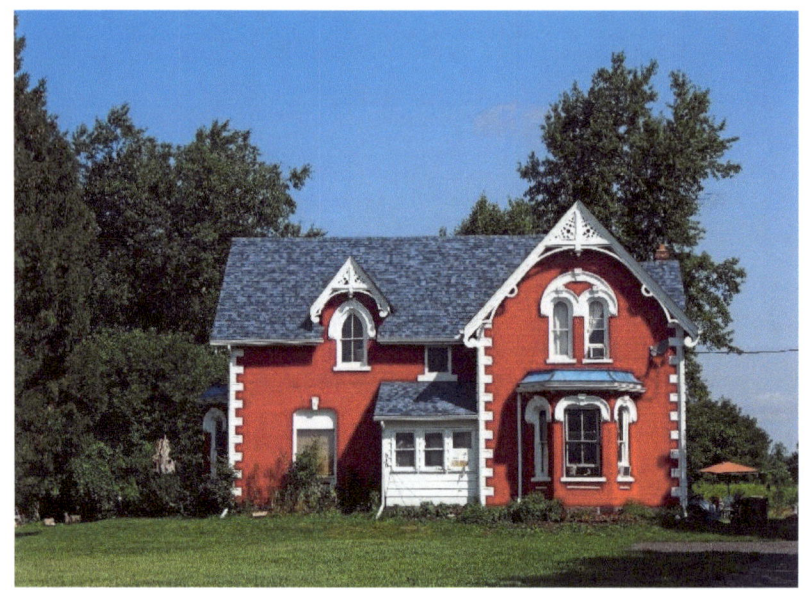

540 King Street East – Gothic – verge board trim, corner quoins, bay window, drip molds with keystones

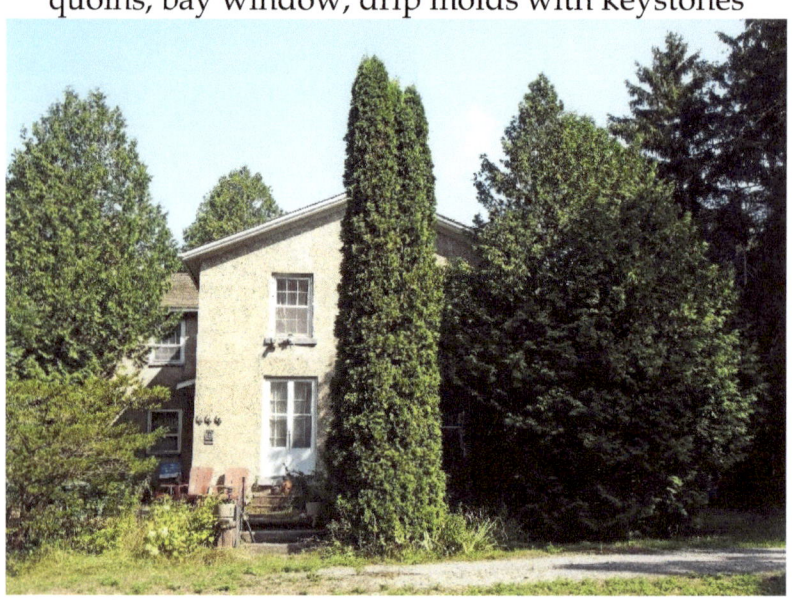

444 King Street East – c. 1835 - Built by the Wright Brothers who imported Angus Cattle from Scotland. It is Gothic Vernacular Farmhouse.

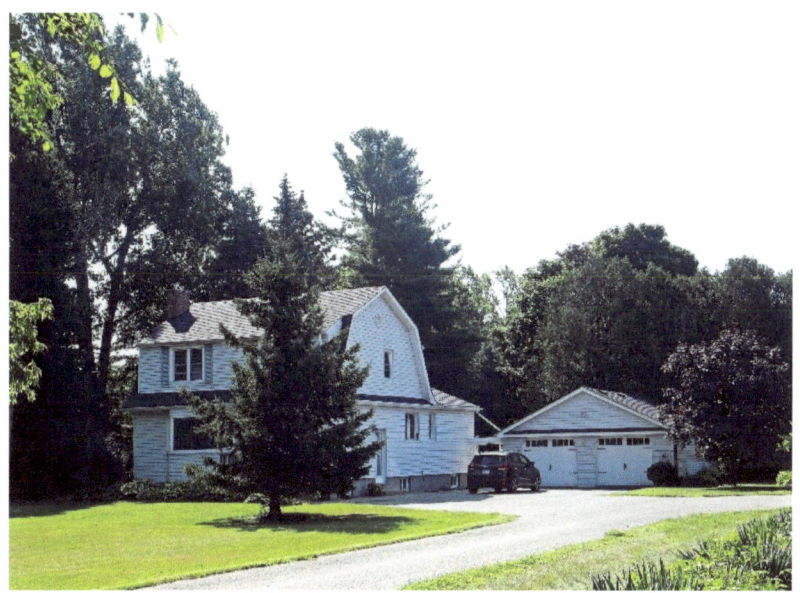

King Street East – Neo-Colonial style, gambrel roof

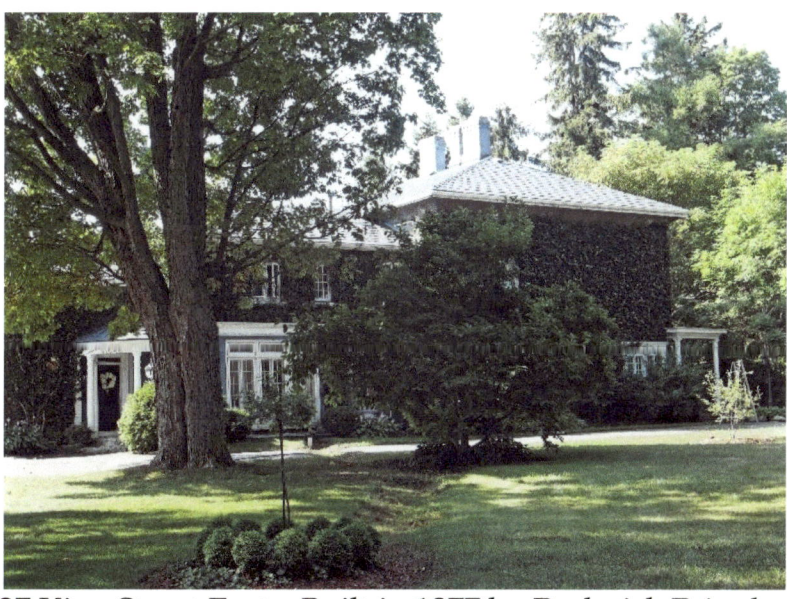

427 King Street East – Built in 1877 by Roderick Pringle, a prominent member of Conservative Party and friend of Sir John A. MacDonald. In 1905 purchased by George Howe of Pittsburgh Steel.

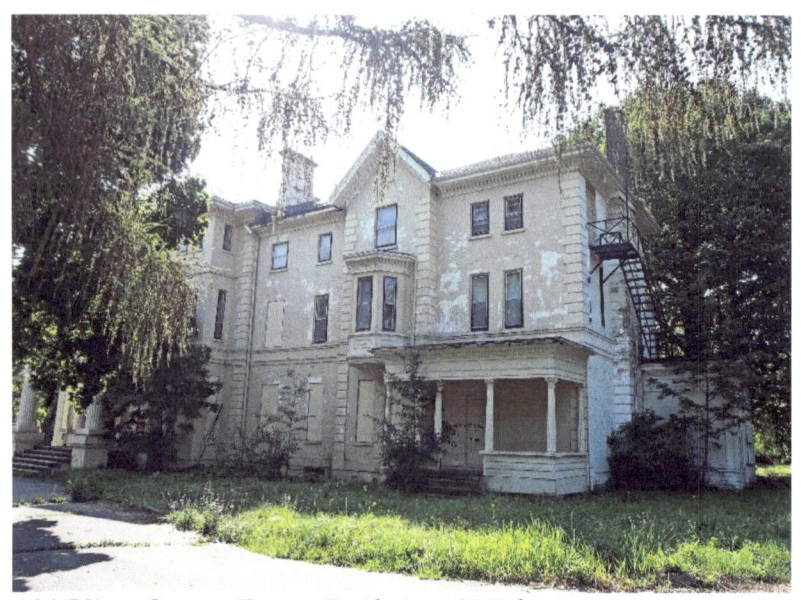

411 King Street East - Built in 1857 for Henry Mason, a director of Cobourg Railway. Architect was Kivas Tully. It is in the High Italianate architectural style with Corinthian capitals on the two storey high columns, a second-floor porch with railing, dentil molding under the eaves, oriel window.

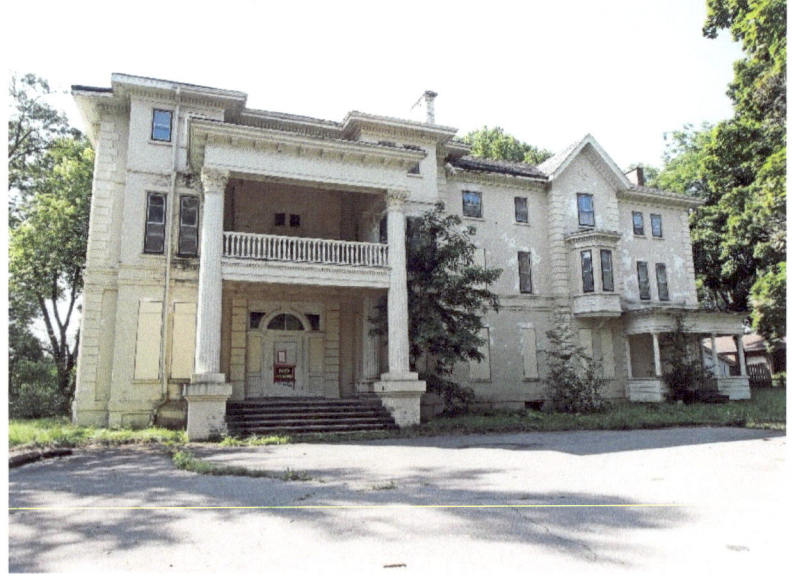

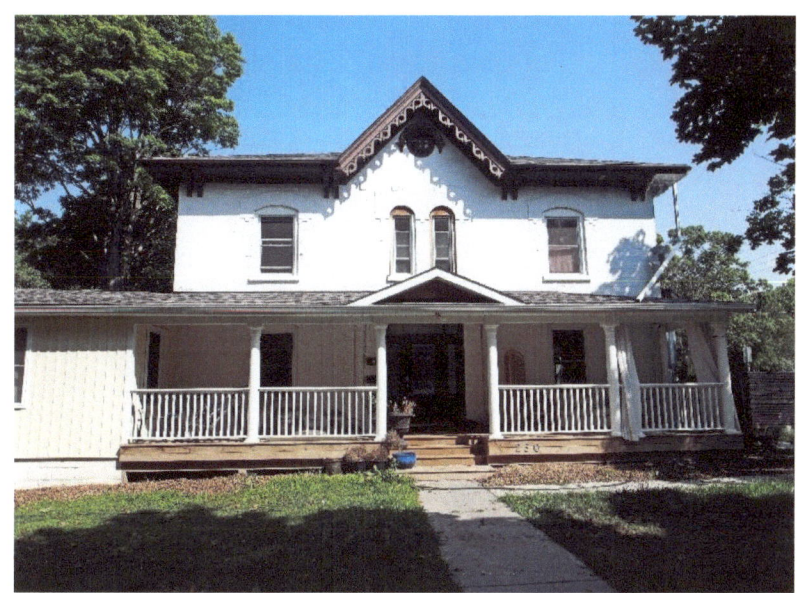

250 King Street East

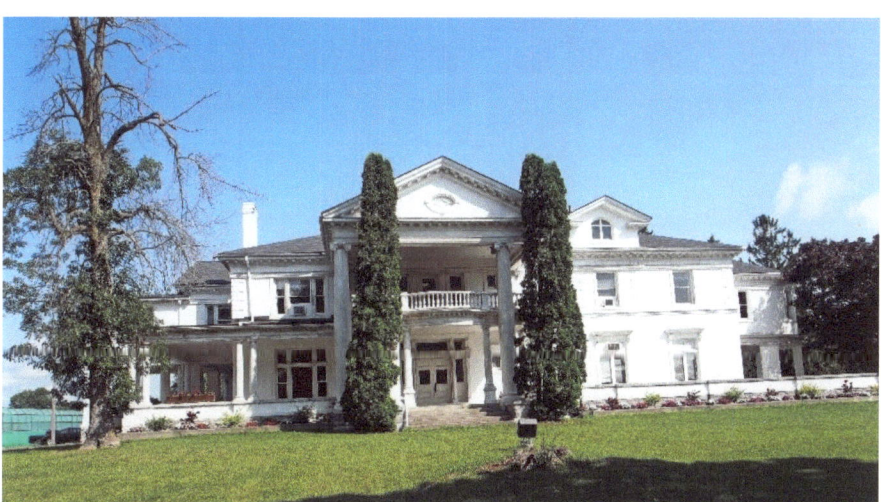

390 King Street East – c. 1878 - Brookside Youth Centre – pediment with decorated tympanum above two-storey veranda supported by Ionic pillars; dentil molding on cornice; lower level veranda has Doric pillars.

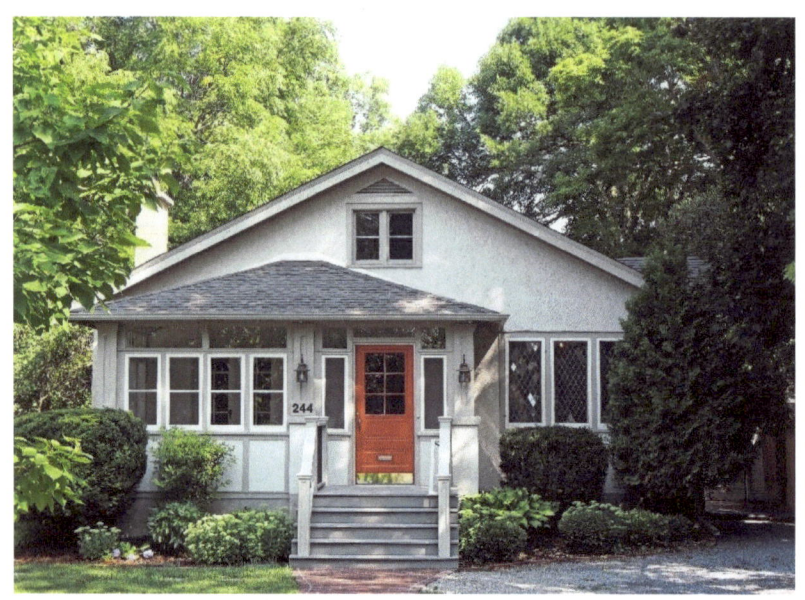

244 King Street East

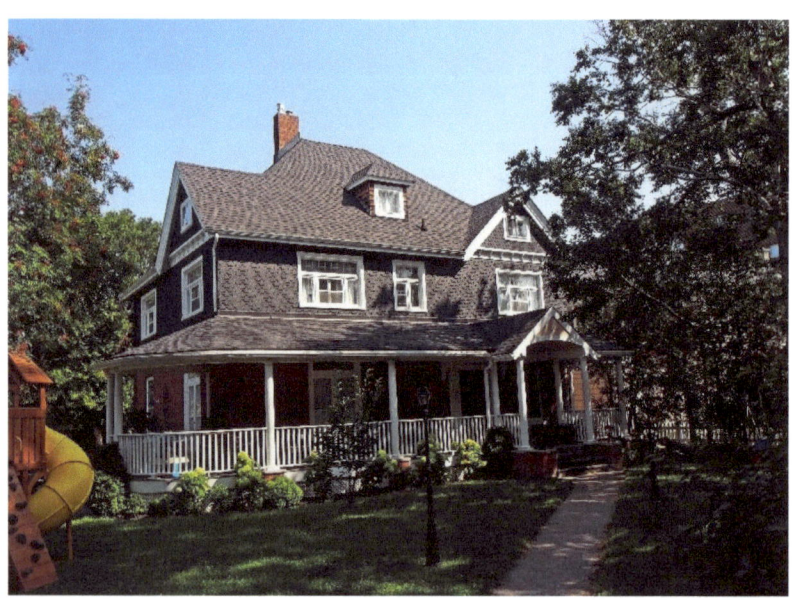

214 King Street East – c. 1891 - Home of George Armour, son
of Chief Justice of Canada (John Armour), from 1910 to 1930s.
Queen Anne Style with irregular plan

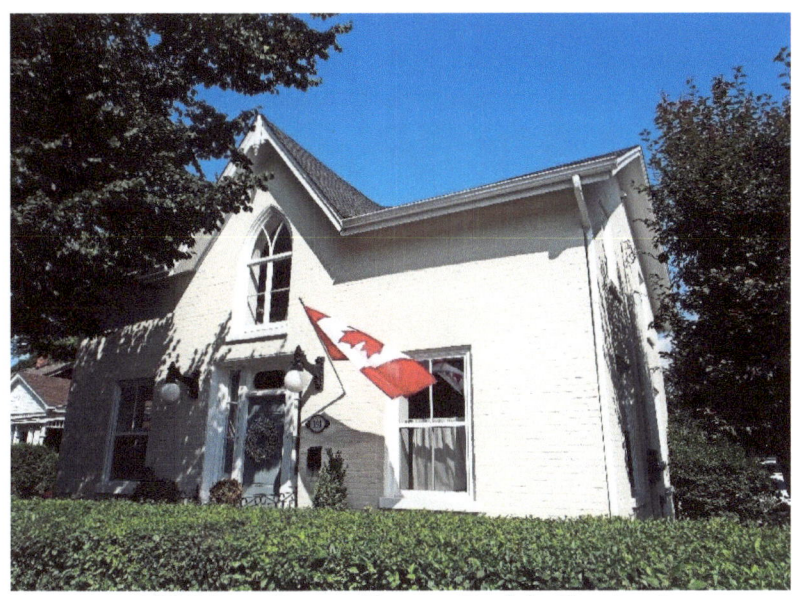

198 King Street East – Gothic Revival

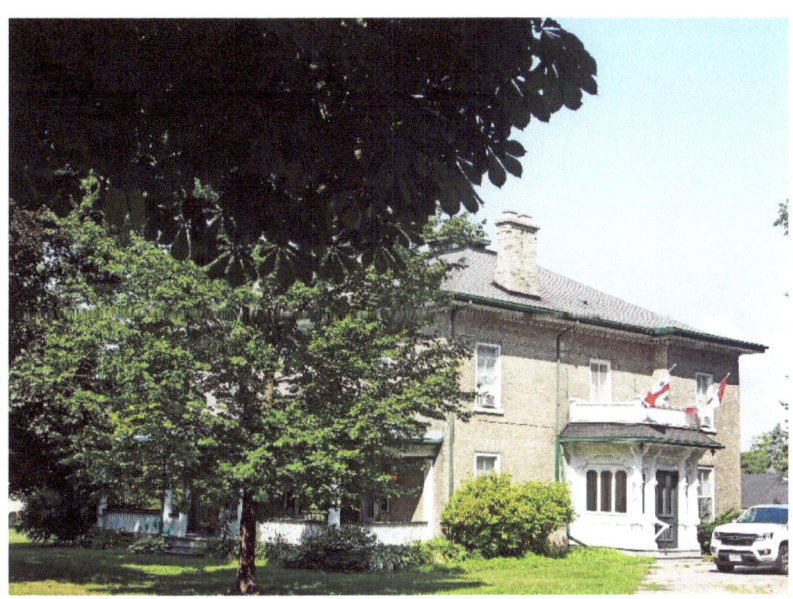

199 King Street East

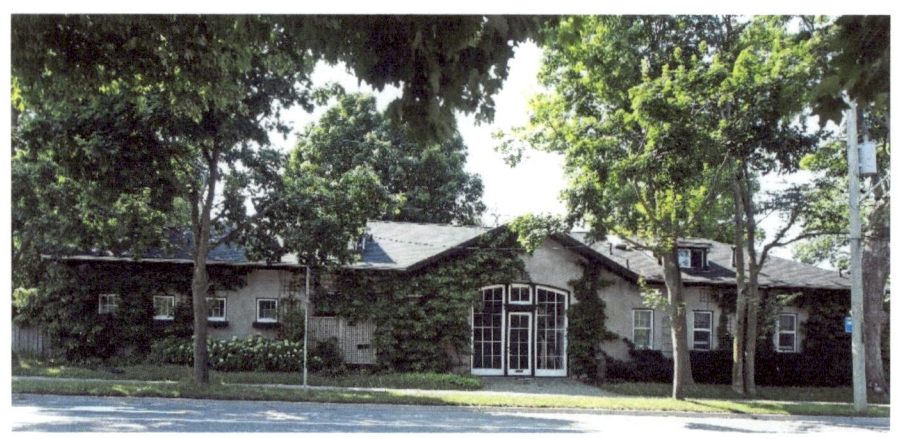

King Street East

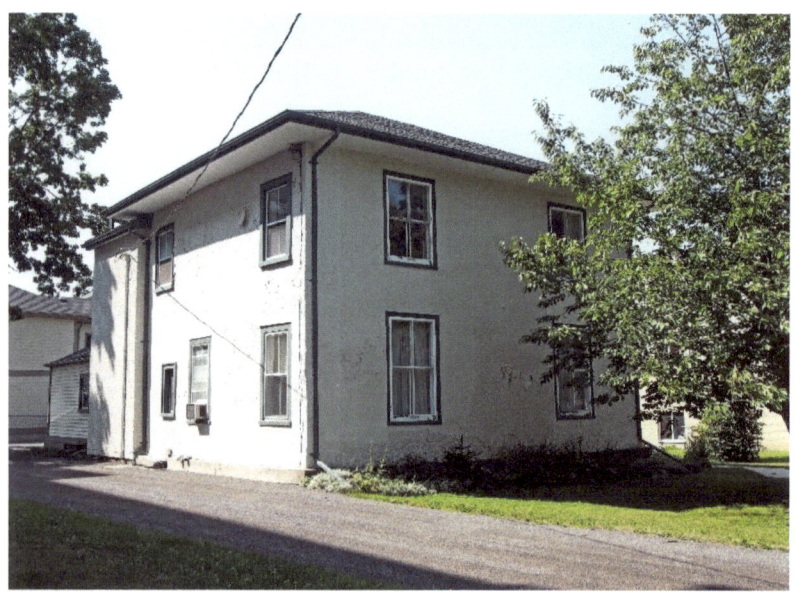

King Street East – hipped roof

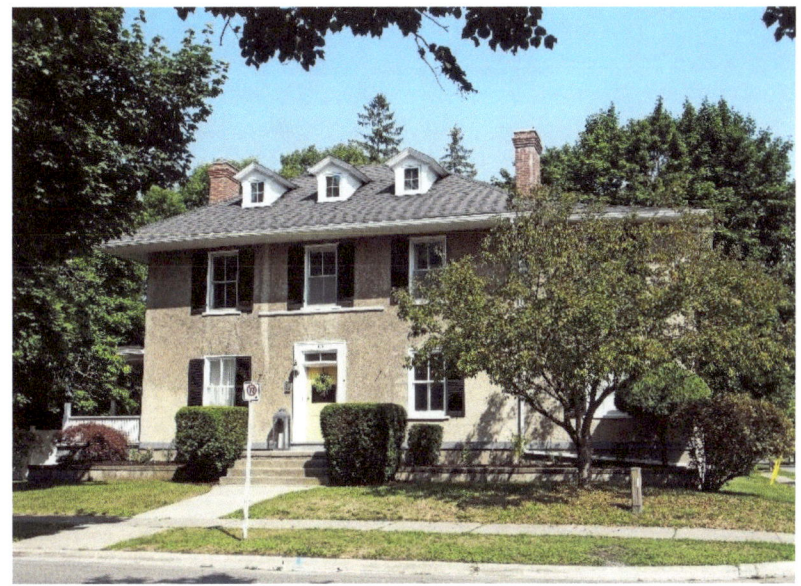

170 King Street East - c. 1840. This residence in the Georgian style was built by Joseph Townsend, and later owned by John Crease Boswell, Cobourg postmaster.

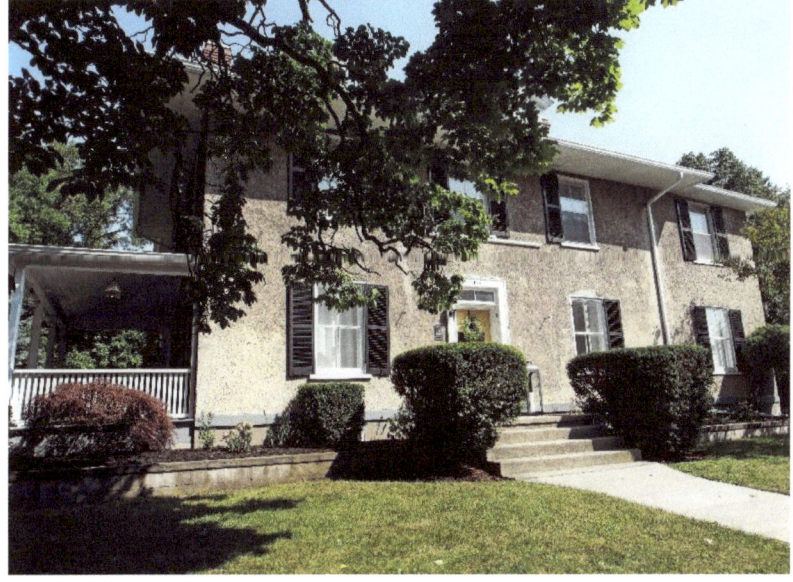

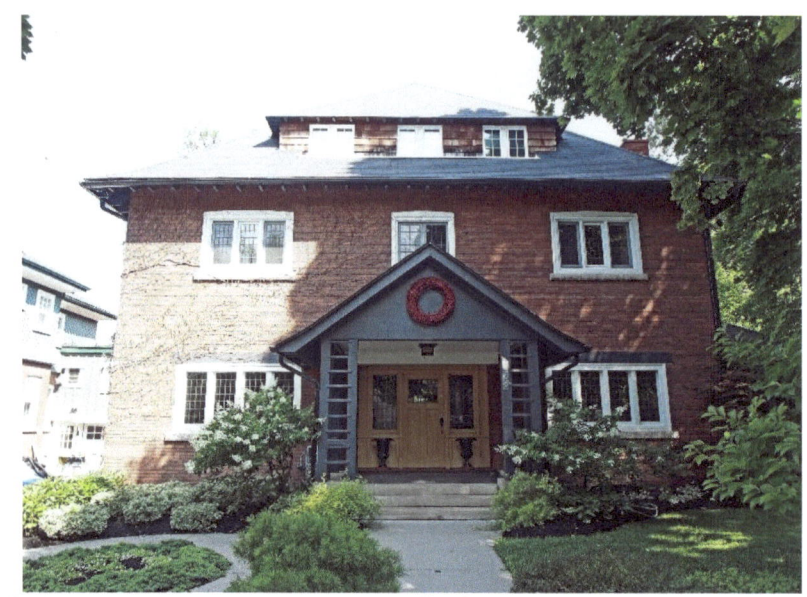

160 King Street East - "New Hall", 1913. English Cottage style of architecture. It was built by Senator Clive Pringle, whose wife was the daughter of Madame Albertini, proprietress of the Arlington Hotel.

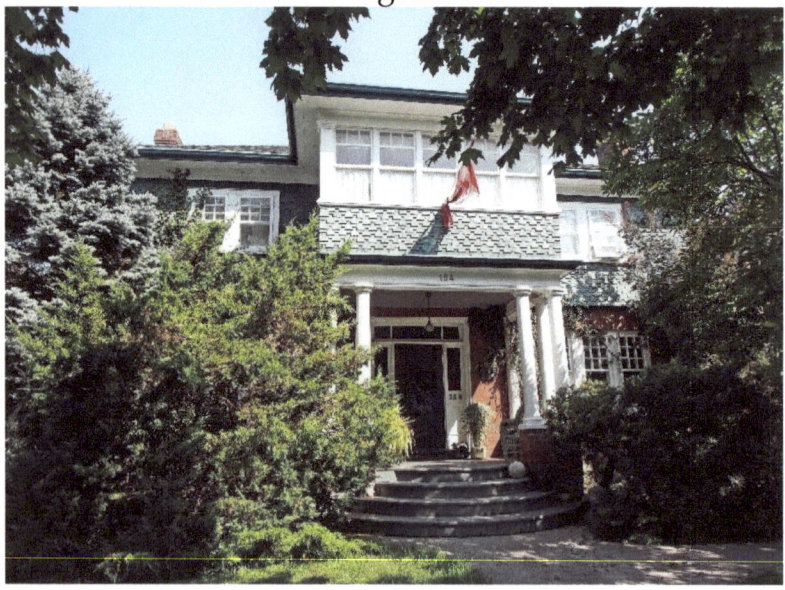

154 King Street East

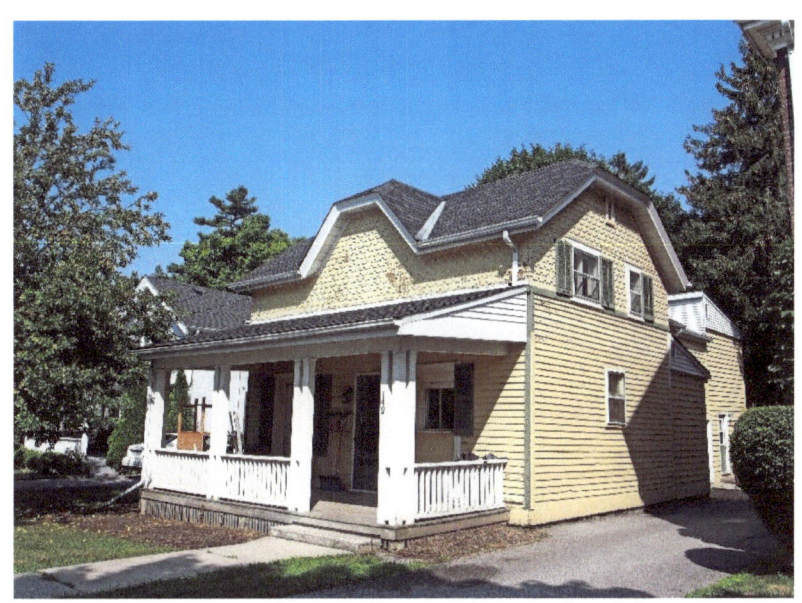

142 King Street East – chipped gables

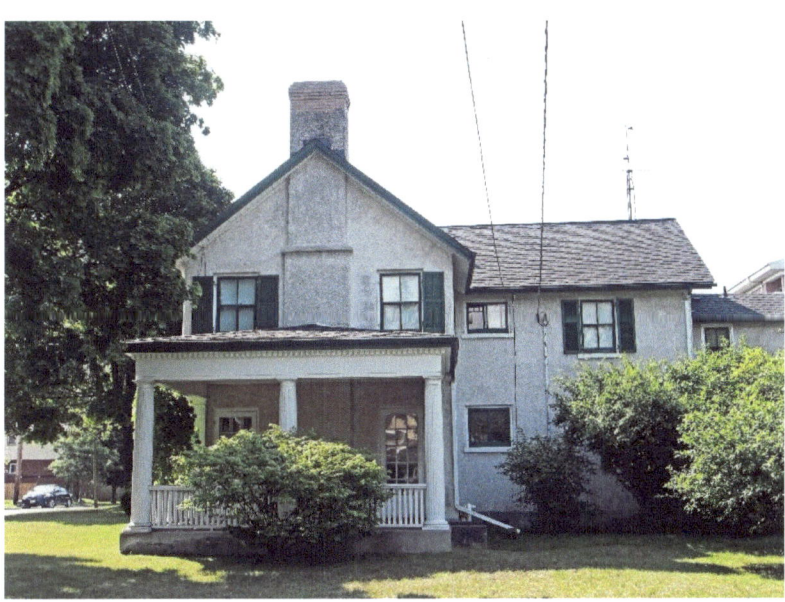

King Street East

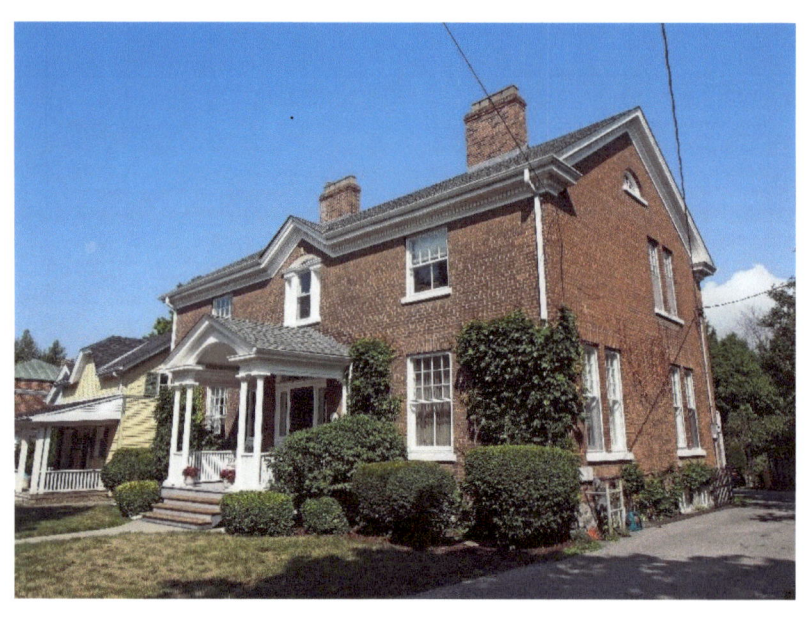

144 King Street East

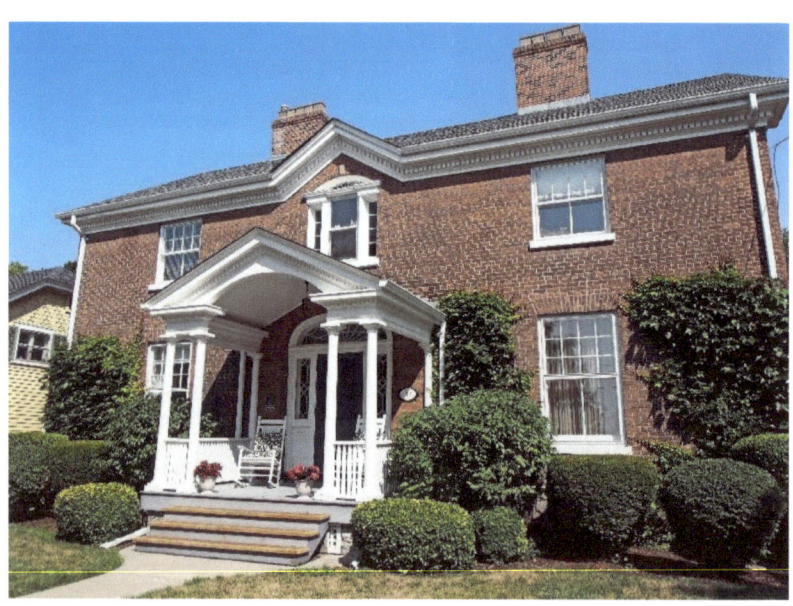

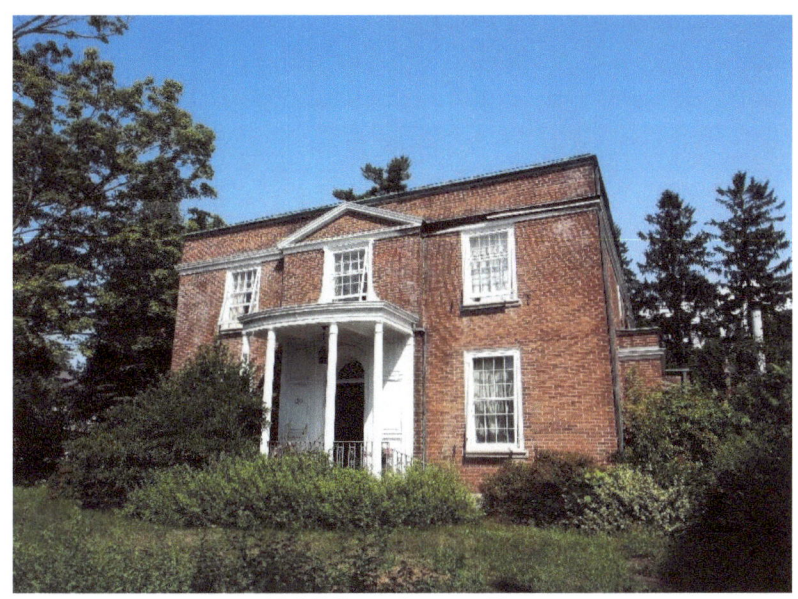

130 King Street East

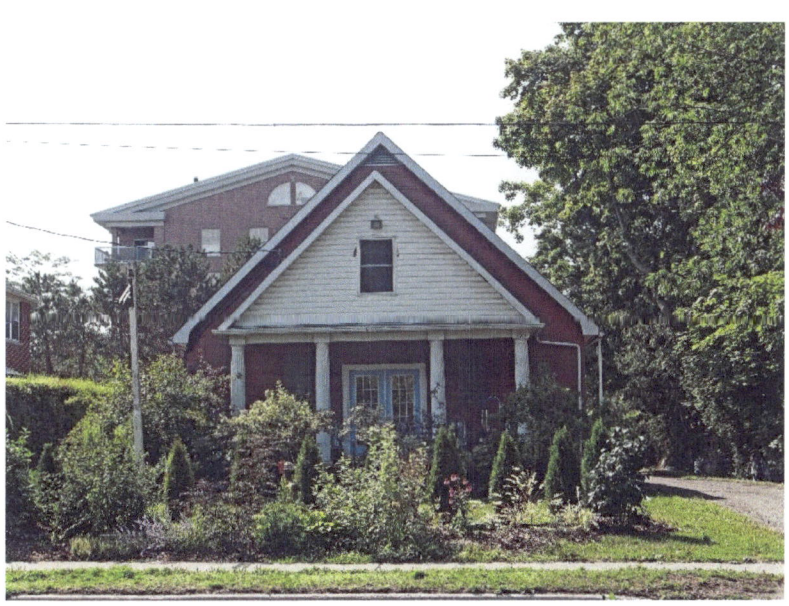

131 King Street East

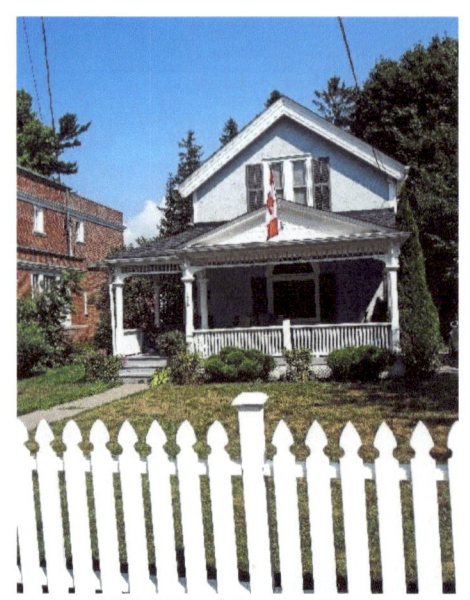

136 King Street East

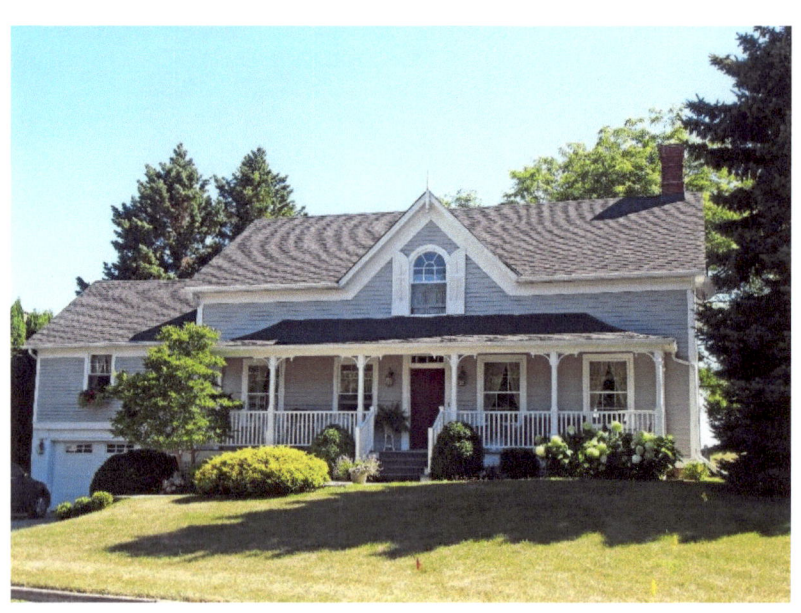

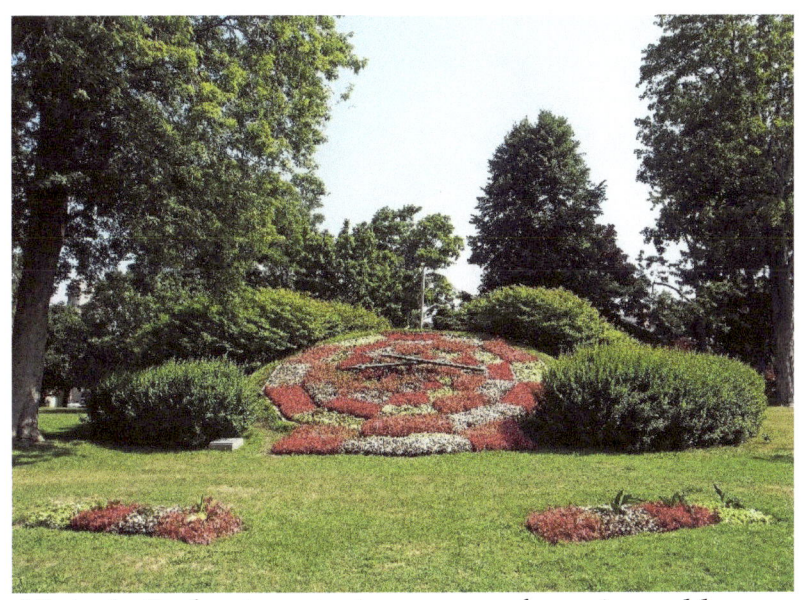

Victoria Park – twenty-two acres of manicured lawns stretching from King Street East to a sandy beach on Lake Ontario

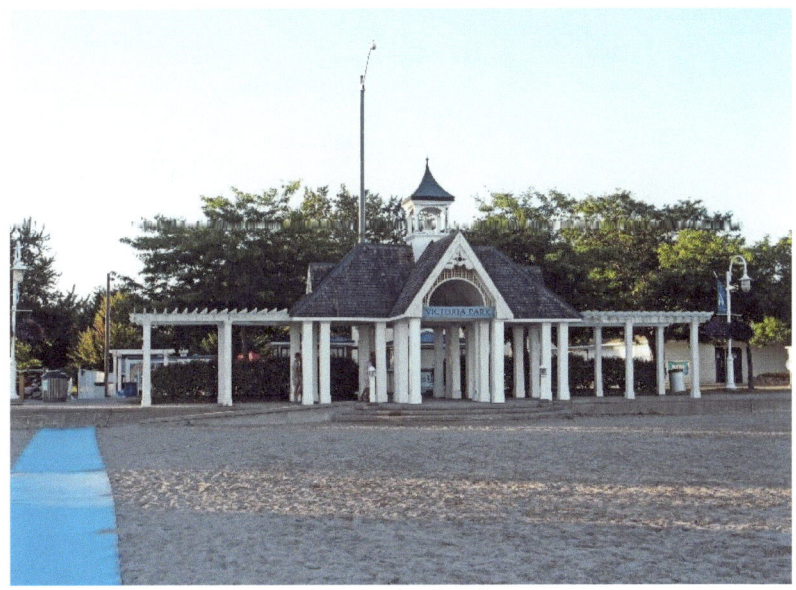

Victoria Park

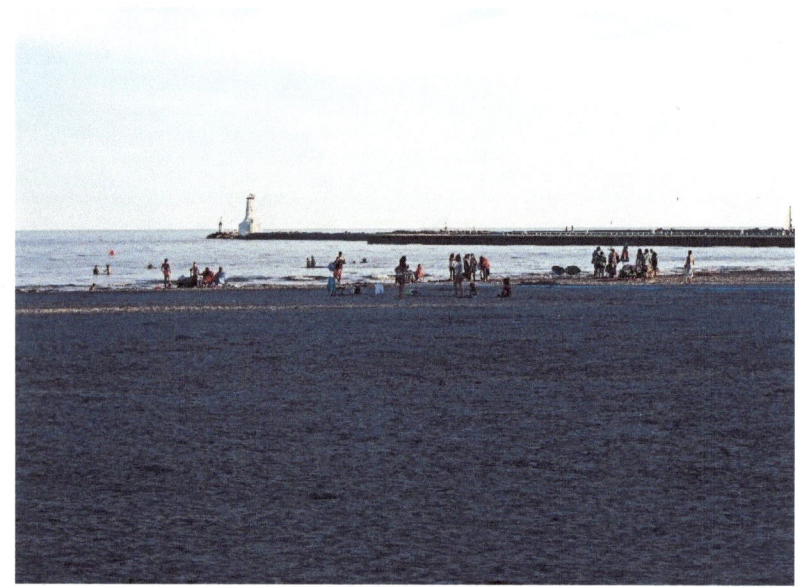

Sand beach on Lake Ontario

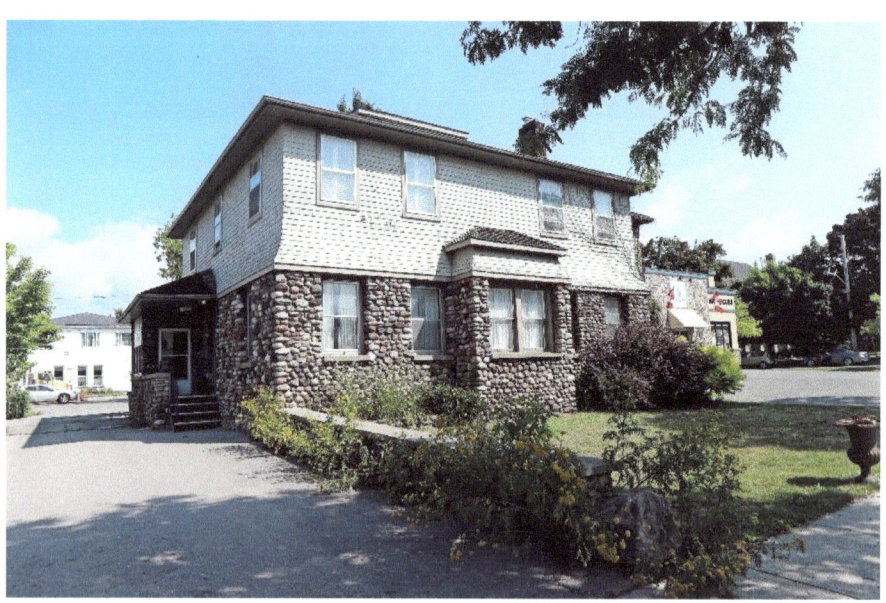

Cobblestones on lower level

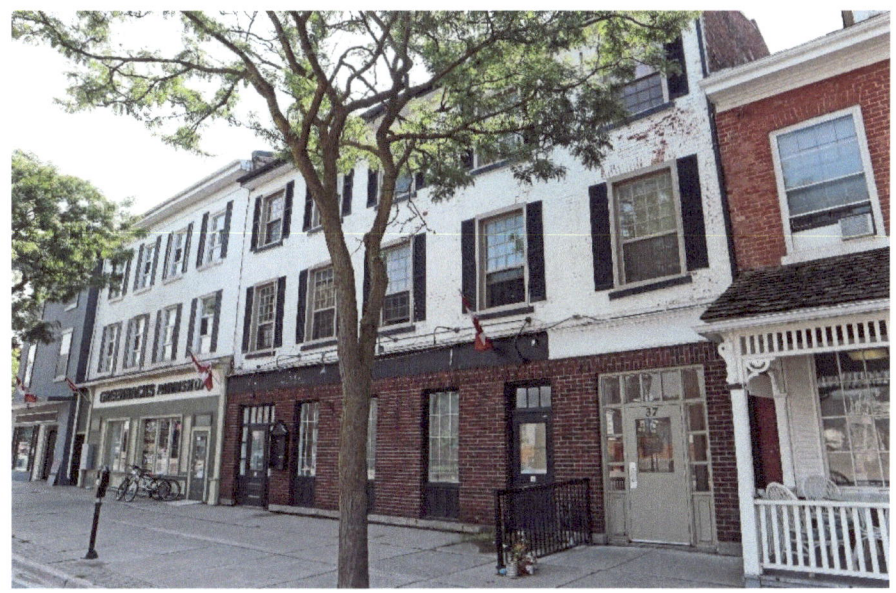

King Street East

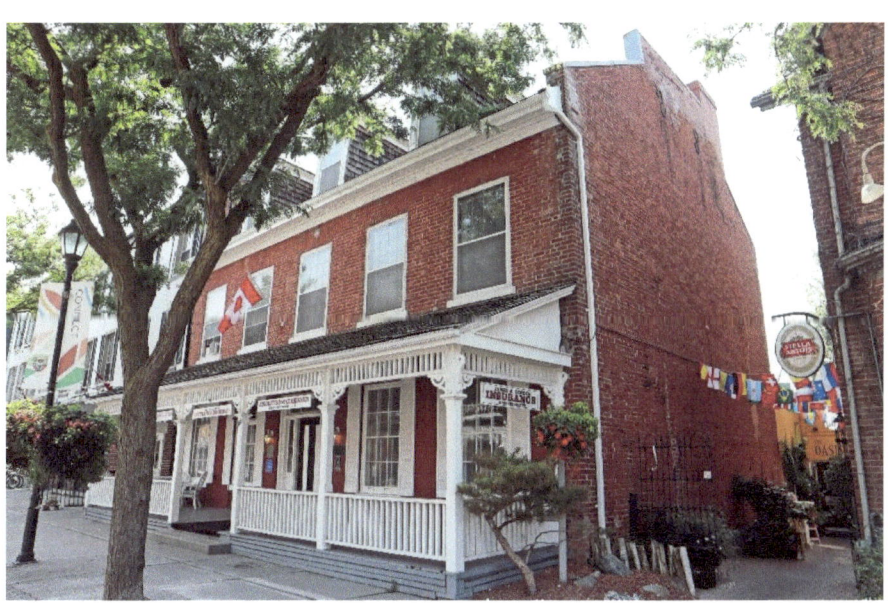

35 King Street East

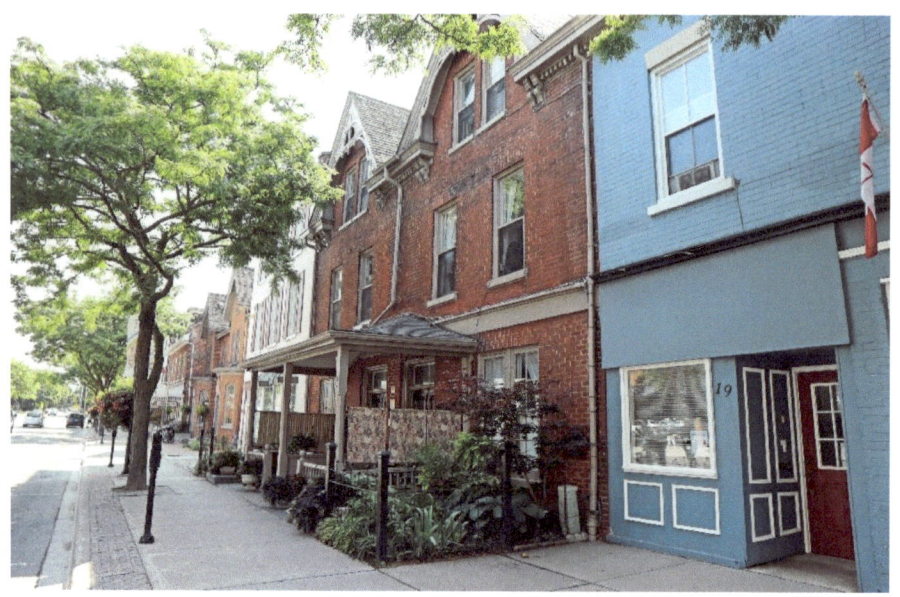

19 King Street East

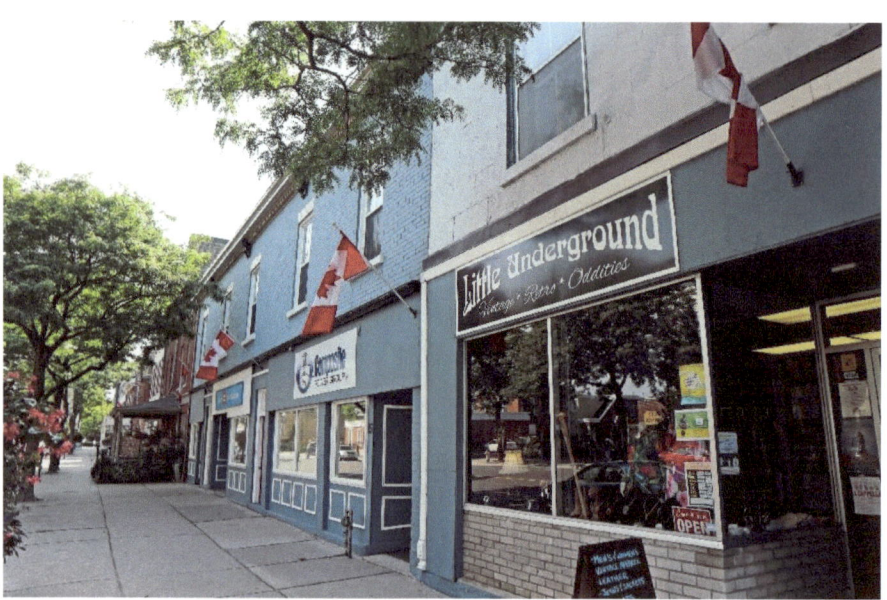

11 King Street East

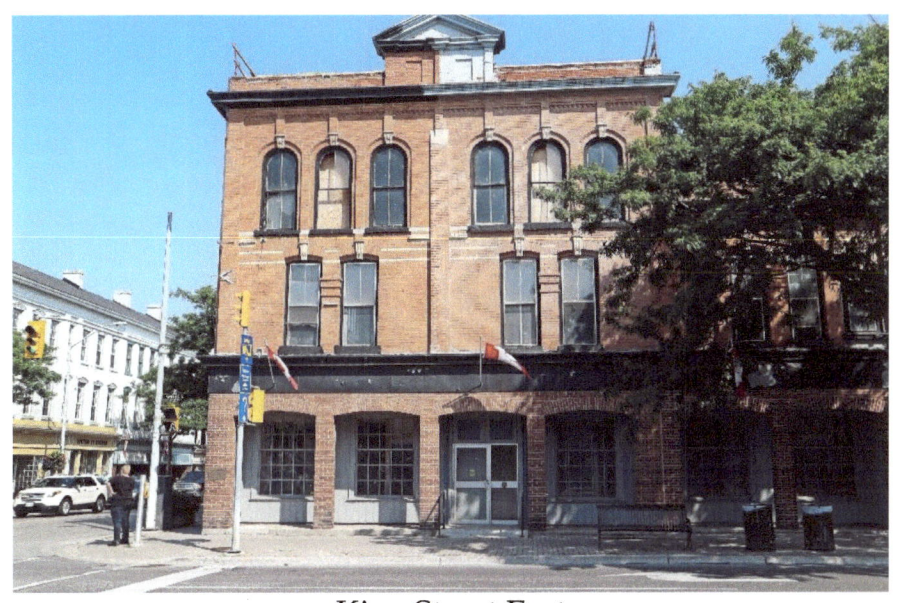

King Street East

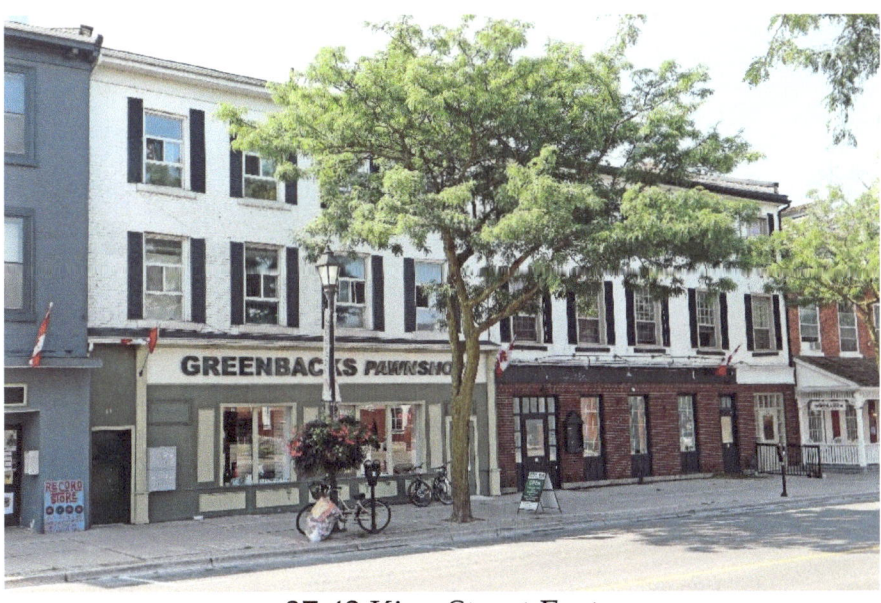

37-43 King Street East

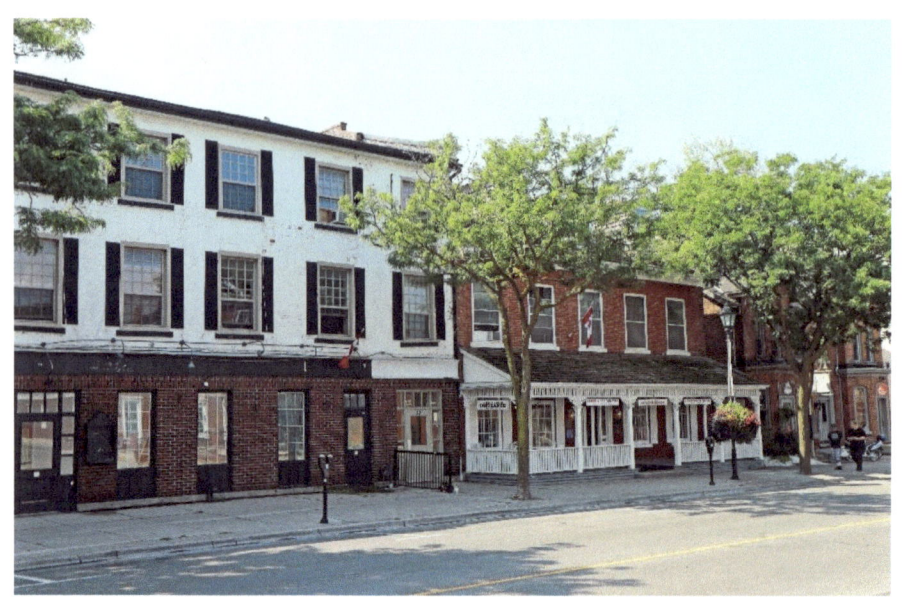

35-37 King Street East – c. 1837 – Georgian style of architecture

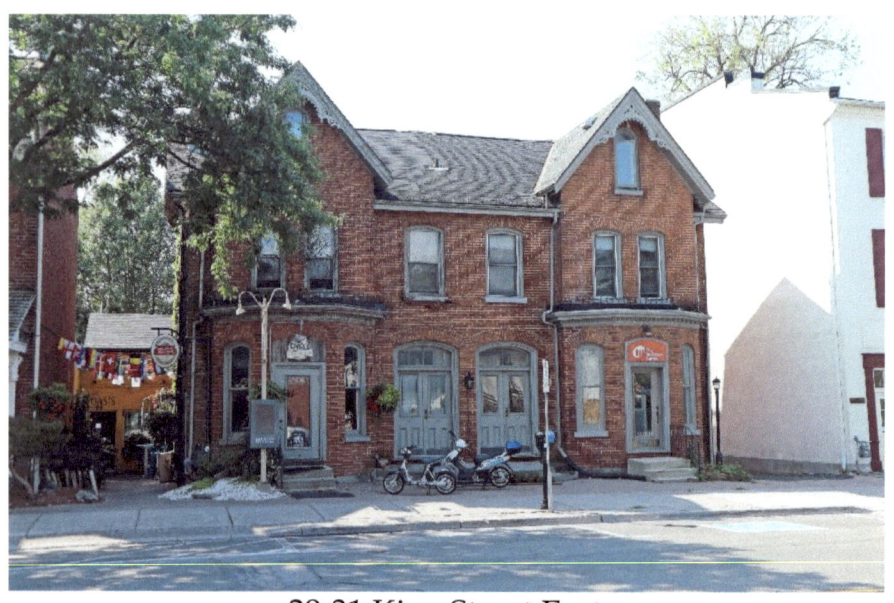

29-31 King Street East

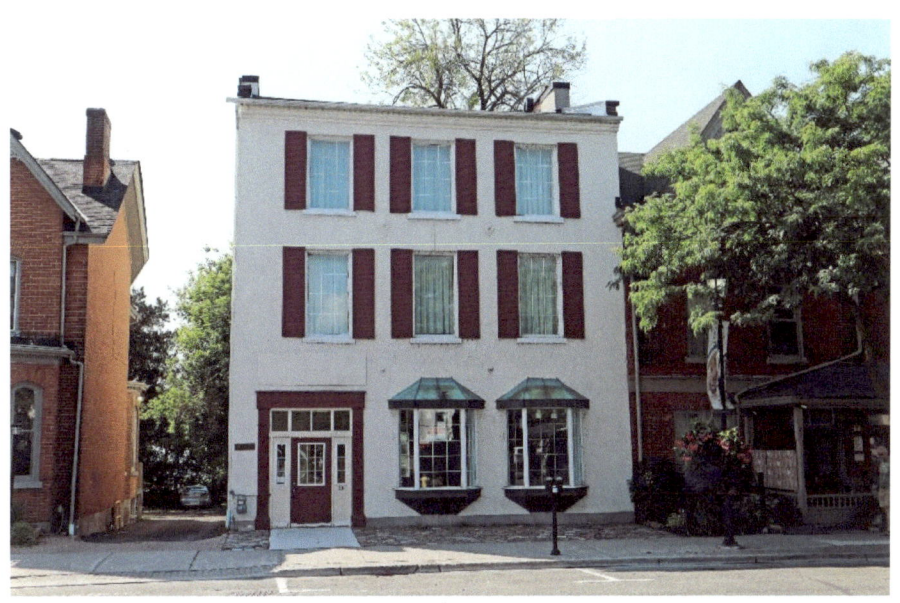

25 King Street East

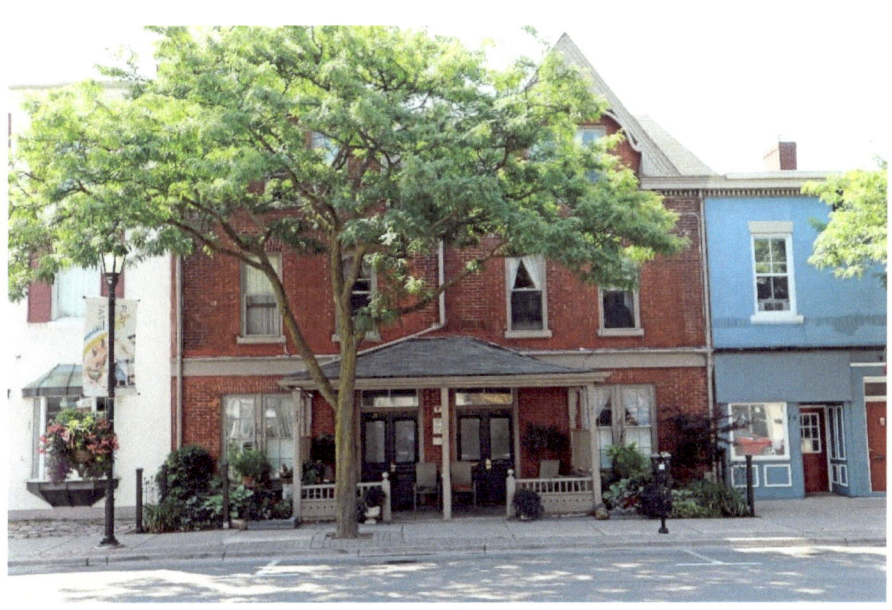

21-23 King Street East

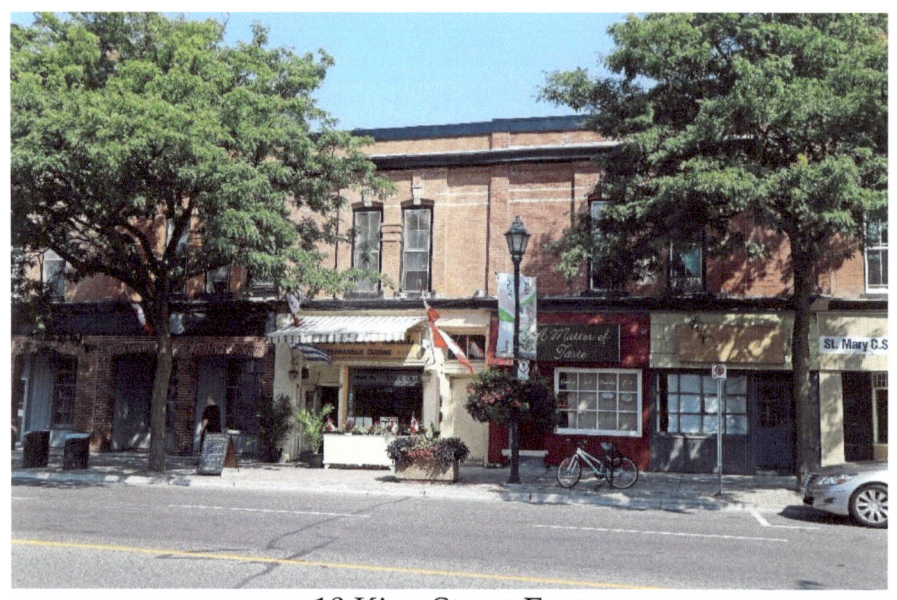

10 King Street East

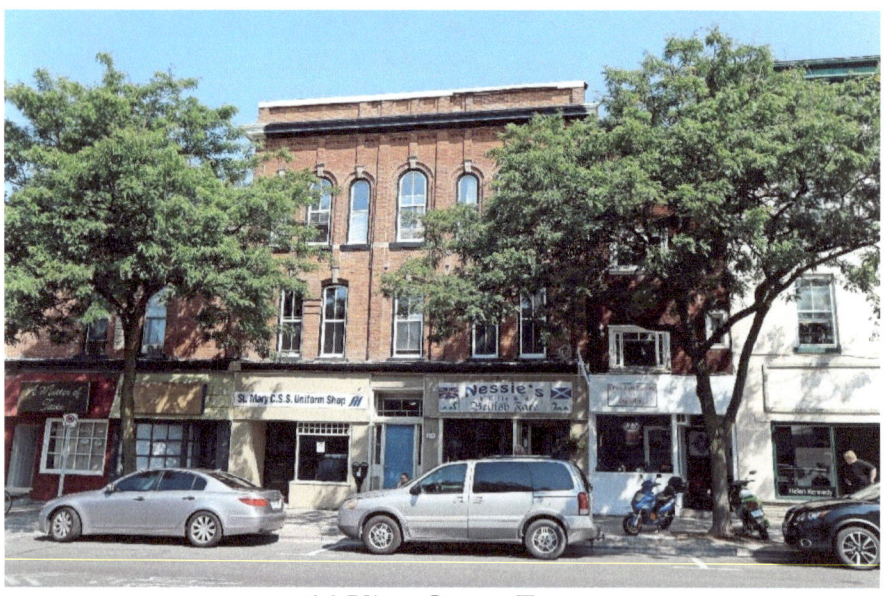

14 King Street East

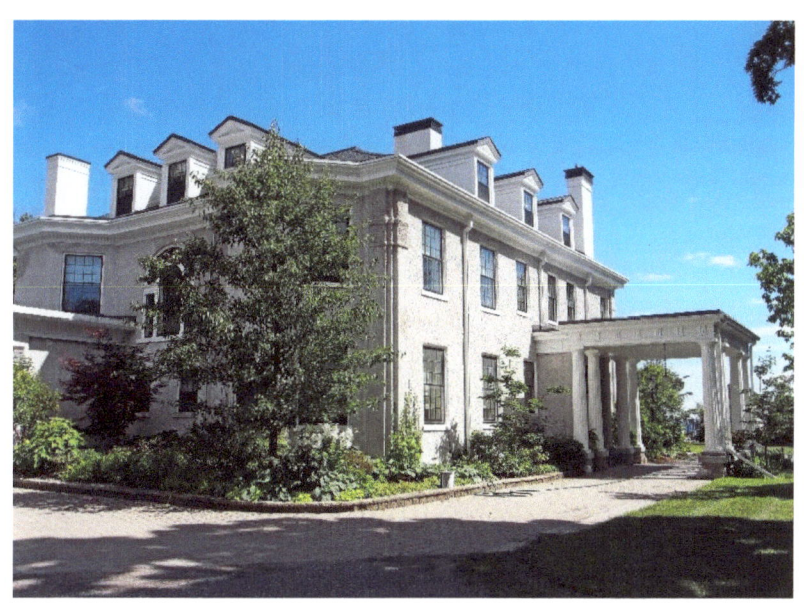

7 Fitzhugh Lane - Ravensworth

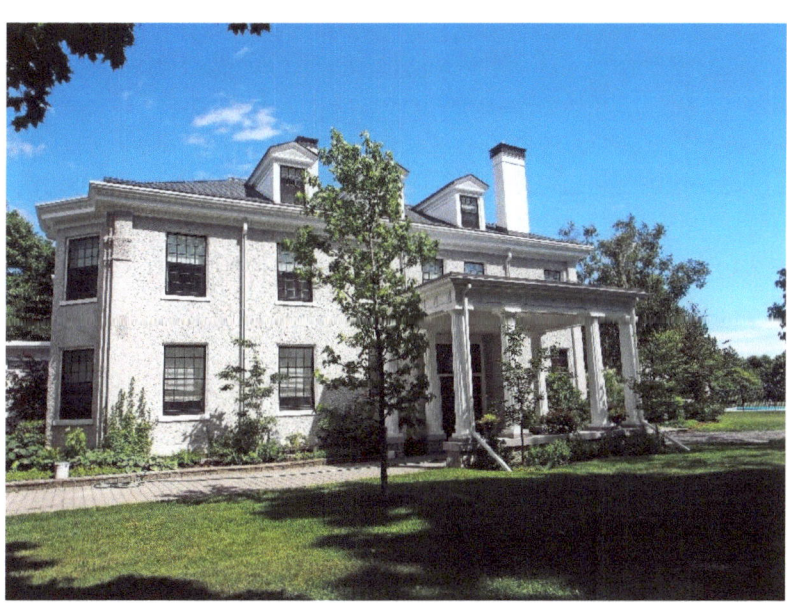

Ravensworth, a waterfront mansion with four bedrooms and four bathrooms, built circa 1897 on Lake Ontario for a distinguished Union officer in the American Civil War. The Colonial Revival-style house sits on 3½ acres at the eastern edge of Cobourg. It is built to symmetrical Georgian proportions and embellished with Greek columns, an imposing portico and a large sunroom with lake views.

In the 19th century the town was known as resort for American steel magnates from Pittsburgh and other centers of the industrial United States. Among those barons travelling north to survey their iron mines near Marmora were members of Emma Shoenberger Fitzhugh's family. She had married a military man thought to be the youngest general in the American Civil War.

Many years after the war ended, Brigadier-General Charles L. Fitzhugh commissioned Ravensworth as a summer estate on 50 acres. Brigadier-General Fitzhugh looked to his roots in an old Virginia family and modelled the new summer getaway on an ancestral plantation house near Fairfax, Virginia.

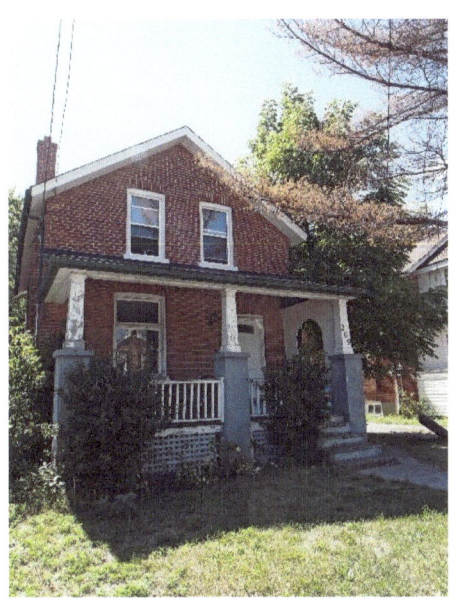

269 William Street

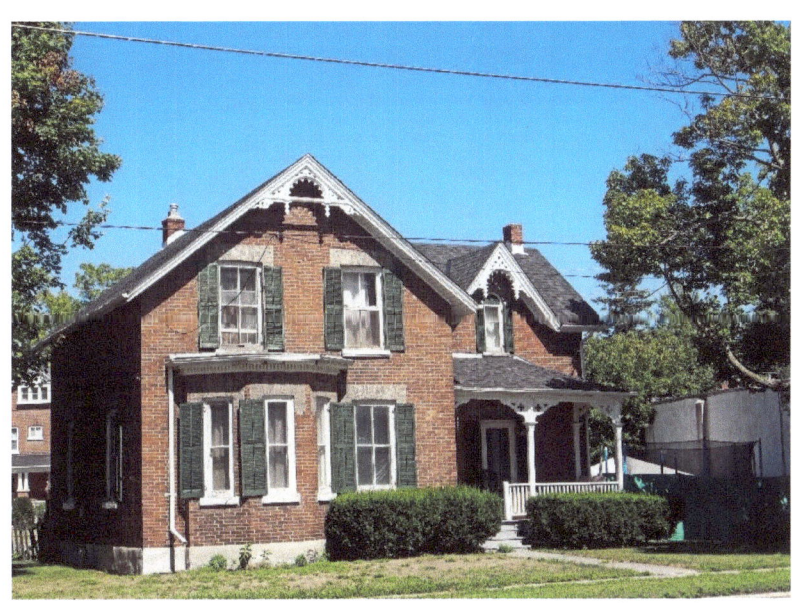

276 William Street – Gothic Revival – verge board trim on gables, shutters

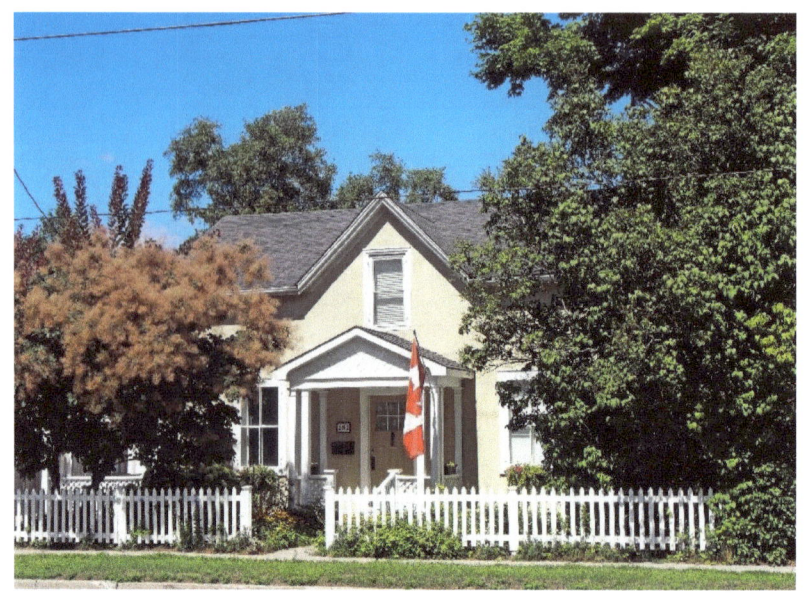

282 William Street

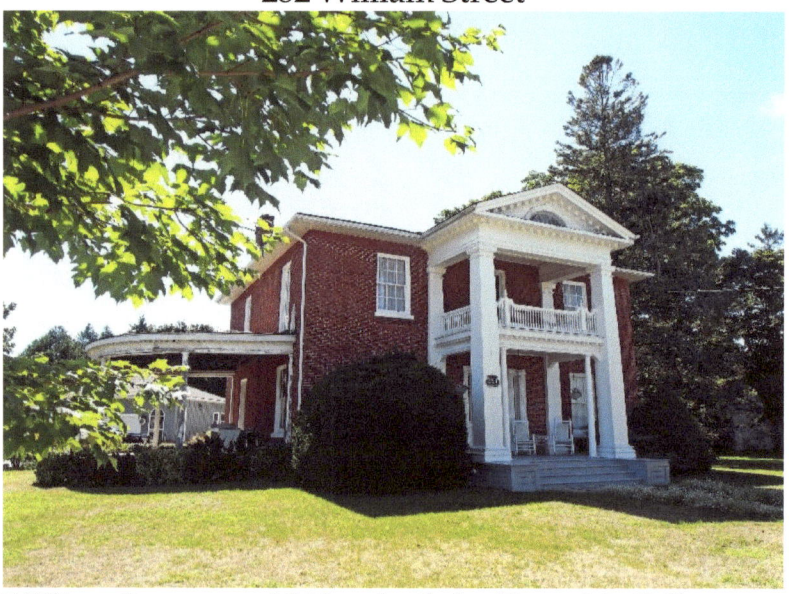

351 William Street – c. 1840s – built by Peter McCallum, a
prominent merchant – Classical Revival style of architecture –
The attractive portico and veranda were added c. 1900. The
porch is supported by four squared Doric columns.

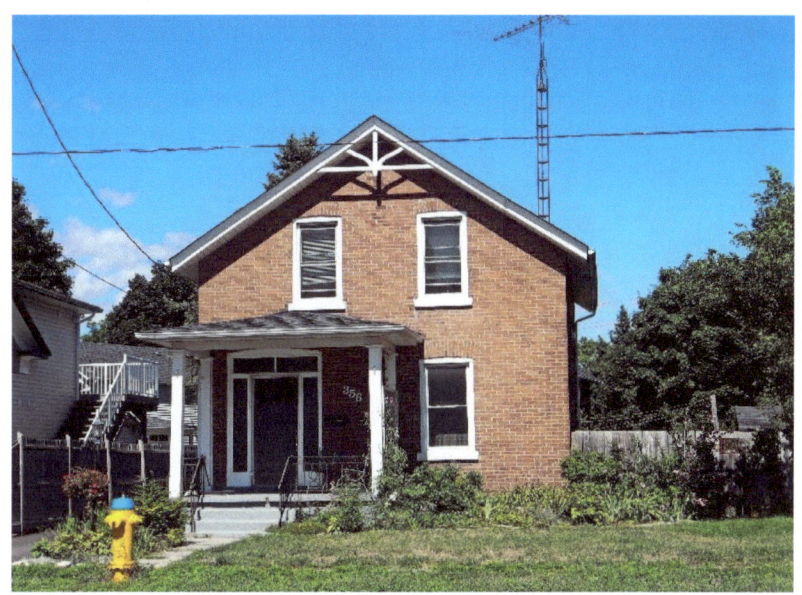

356 William Street

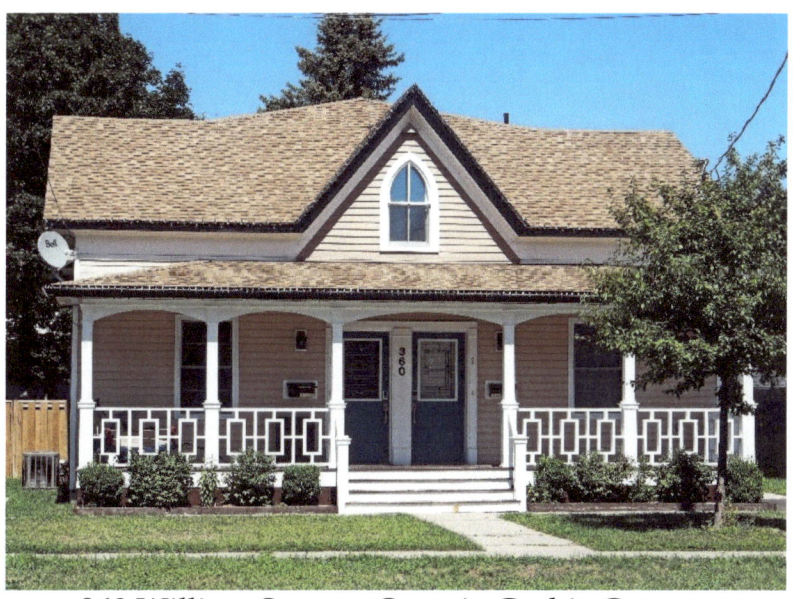

360 William Street – Ontario Gothic Cottage

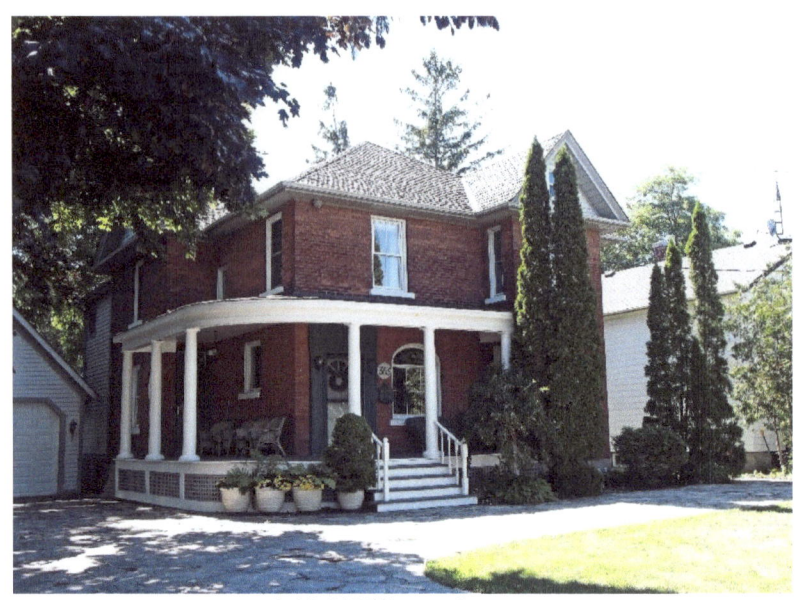

363 William Street

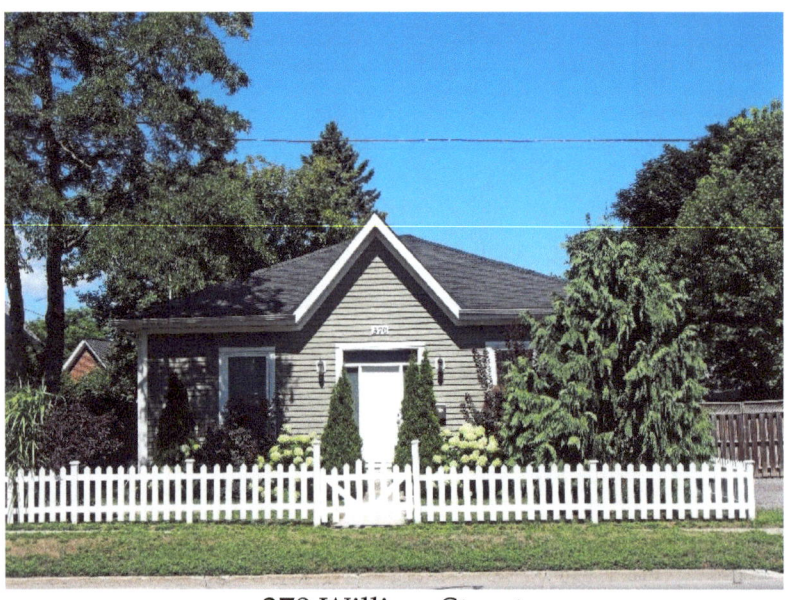

370 William Street

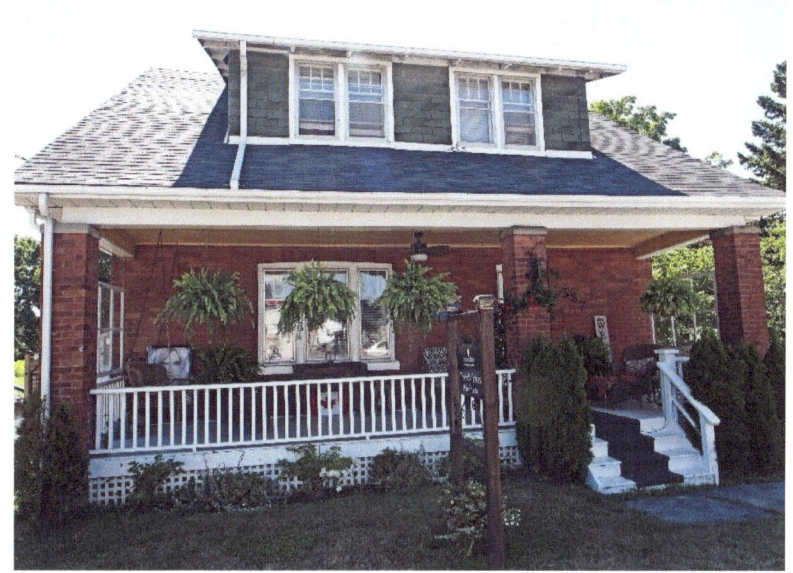

387 William Street – shed dormer

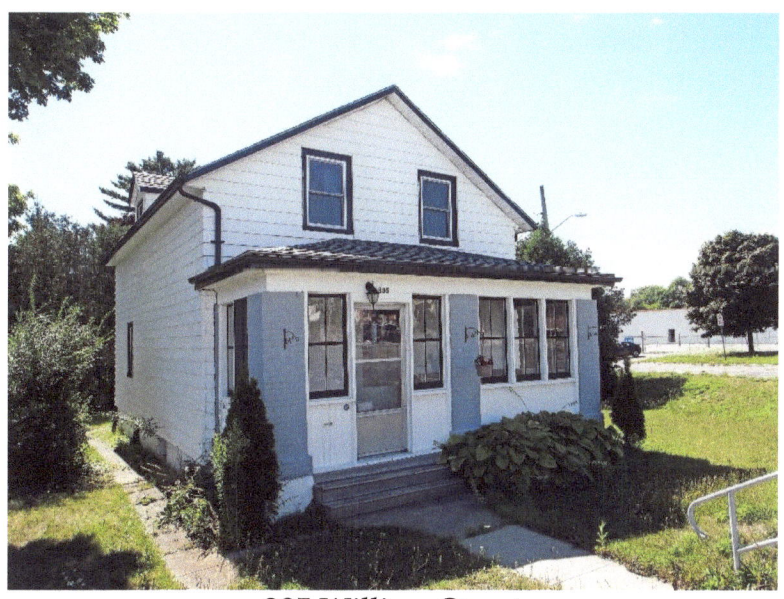

395 William Street

# Other Books by Barbara Raue

Coins of Gold
Arrows, Indians and Love
The Life and Times of Barbara
The Cromwell Family Book
Laura Secord Discovered
Daddy Where Are You?

Montana Series
Book 1: Montana Dream
Book 2: Life on the Montana Frontier
Book 3: Montana to Boston and Back
Book 4: Montana Sons Go to War
Book 5: Montana Sons Return from War

Visit Barbara's website to view all of her books
http://barbararaue.ca

www.ingramcontent.com/pod-product-compliance
Lightning Source LLC
Chambersburg PA
CBHW041105180526
45172CB00001B/118